RELATIONAL MASKS

Removing the

Barriers That

Keep Us Apart

Russell Willingham

InterVarsity Press
Downers Grove, Illinois

InterVarsity Press
P.O. Box 1400, Downers Grove, IL 60515-1426
World Wide Web: www.ivpress.com
E-mail: mail@ivpress.com

InterVarsity Press® is the bookpublishing division of InterVarsity Christian Fellowship/USA®, a student movement active on campus at hundreds of universities, colleges and schools of nursing in the United States of America, and a member movement of the International Fellowship of Evangelical Students. For information about local and regional activities, write Public Relations Dept., InterVarsity Christian Fellowship/USA, 6400 Schroeder Rd., P.O. Box 7895, Madison, WI 537077895, or visit the IVCF website at <www.ivcf.org>.

The stories that appear in this book are based on the lives of real people. Names and details have been changed to protect the confidentiality of these individuals.

Design: Cindy Kiple

Images: F. Schussler/PhotoLink/Getty Images

ISBN 0-8308-3251-3

Printed in the United States of America ∞

Library of Congress Cataloging-in-Publication Data

Willingham, Russell.
 Relational masks: removing the barriers that keep us apart/
 Russell Willingham.
     p. cm.
 Includes bibliographical references.
 ISBN 0-8308-3251-3 (pbk.: alk. paper)
 1. Interpersonal relations—Religious aspects—Christianity. I.
 Title
 BV4597.52.W55 2004
 248.4—dc22

                                                                    2004011516

P	19	18	17	16	15	14	13	12	11	10	9	8	7	6	5	4	3	2	1
Y	19	18	17	16	15	14	13	12	11	10	09	08	07	06	05	04				

This book is lovingly dedicated to

the men and women of New Creation Ministries.

For a decade I've had the privilege of walking with you

through profound pain and unspeakable joy.

But I am the one who has been taught and

blessed in ways you will never know.

CONTENTS

ACKNOWLEDGMENTS

My wife has always been my number-one supporter, and this book is no exception. Without her and her prayers it wouldn't have happened. There are three others who have been crucial in the process: Della Ortiz, Donna Hamm and Kathryn Belmont. These three women have encouraged me and have been (along with my wife) the intercessors who prayed it into existence.

I want to thank Scott Rungwerth for always praying and asking about the project. Your genuine interest in the book was a great encouragement to me. Thank you, Ferral Henderson of Peoples Church, for letting me use your office to write. It was a quiet place to work when no other place was. Thank you, Connie Helbling, for donating the computer I wrote the book with. If fruit comes from this, you get some of the credit.

Thank you, Virginia Muir, for your editing expertise and your encouragement. I'm so grateful to Al Hsu and the publishing committee of InterVarsity Press for their confidence in me and this project. Your vision helped make it happen. Thank you, Dan Allender, for writing about relating styles in *The Wounded Heart*. It was your work that got me thinking. Thank you, Jonathan Olford, for your friendship and mentoring. You have shaped me more than you know. Thanks to all the clients, supporters and volunteers at New Creation Ministries who frequently asked, "How's the book coming?"

Last, thank you, Lord Jesus, for guiding me. I did what you commanded (Matthew 10:27). Lord, use these words to answer the questions that broken people ask and to transform them. You know that our generation is desperate for truth. Let this little message be a part of your healing response.

PREFACE

The story is told of a child psychologist who liked doing repairs on his home. One Saturday he was putting the finishing touches on a driveway. The concrete was still wet as he gently smoothed it with his trowel. A few feet away stood a neighborhood boy, watching him as he worked.

Across the street was a neighbor mowing his lawn. For years this neighbor had listened as the doctor went on and on about how he loved working with kids. He kept his eye on the doctor and the little boy, wondering if there might be trouble. Sure enough, as soon as the doctor finished his work and stood back to admire it, the boy made his move. He jumped into the cement and ran tromping up one side and down the other.

When the boy jumped out the doctor grabbed him and began swatting his behind. The man across the street was quite amazed at the doctor's response. As the boy ran home crying and dripping wet cement, the neighbor called across the street, "Hey, I thought you *loved* kids, Henry."

"I *do* love kids," the doctor replied, "but in the abstract, not in the concrete."

Now, before you tell me to call Child Protective Services, consider the point of the story. The good doctor is like many of us. He makes many claims about what he believes, but his interactions with others don't match what he says.

I spend my days counseling Christians from all walks of life who struggle with different issues. One thing is consistent: the biblical beliefs they hold are quite different from the way they do relationships. I see pastors who are unkind to their spouse and kids; women who lead wonderful Bible studies but are verbally abusive to their husbands; people on church staffs who bicker and fight with each other; men and women who secretly indulge in everything from pornography to out-of-control eating or spending.

Why do we *do* this stuff? Are we hypocrites? Is it because we're not really saved? Is it because we haven't prayed or read as we should? Here is the answer: *We don't really know ourselves.* Hidden beliefs and relational masks hamper our ability to be intimate. Relational masks aren't just "phony fronts." They are styles of relating that we often construct in childhood to protect us from pain. They are a complex grouping of attitudes and behaviors unique to each of us. These relational masks now serve as walls in our adult lives, cutting us off from deeper levels of knowing and being known.

Relational masks aren't just "phony fronts." They are styles of relating that we often construct in childhood to protect us from pain.

Relational masks are difficult to see in ourselves because, as far as we're concerned, the way we relate is "just the way we are." We either don't see anything wrong with it or we work to change some other areas of our lives that leave the masks intact. We read another book, go to another conference or promise God we'll do better next time, yet our relational masks remain.

Many of us have a robust evangelical theology but have problems being intimate with God, self and others. Avoiders and Aggressors rarely deal with anything, but often go after someone else to take the heat off themselves. Self-Blamers are quick to hate all their failures and weaknesses but rarely do anything effective to deal with them.

Though I am experienced working with people and understanding their issues, even that isn't my qualification. My qualification for speaking on this subject comes from my own failure, struggle and confusion. I have served God for years in all kinds of ministry settings, all the while having an awful time relating in my marriage, struggling with my self-image or fighting a variety of fears and doubts.

Yet Jesus has been very gracious to me. He has been showing me what is at work in my own heart that keeps dumping me onto the floor. It has been (and sometimes still is) a painful journey, but I have seen God strip away layer after layer of unbelief, rebellion and pain. As I am learning about how wonderful, yet deceptive, my own heart can be, I've begun seeing similar things in others. As I've shared these thoughts with open-minded Christians, I've seen phenomenal changes happen in their lives.

Some may have no interest in what this book offers. They may believe they are fine as they are or that it's too late for them to change. Neither is true. God has an amazing plan for what you can become and accomplish. You can be like the majority of Jesus' followers and focus on theology or on living a respectable lifestyle. Or you can join those who are determined to let Jesus reveal, fill and own every part of them, no matter what the cost.

I invite you to come with me and learn more about Jesus and about yourself. The road may get bumpy and scary, but it's the right one. Everyone who plants his feet on this trail eventually makes it home. If you choose that other path you'll have lots of company, but you won't like where it takes you. If you're ready for some answers, you will find them on the road ahead.

1

THE STRONGHOLD OF RELATIONAL MASKS

I've discovered something after years of working with people: Almost every Christian struggles with dishonesty at some level. The scary thing is, we can see it clearly in others but miss it in ourselves. Yet Scripture assumes that each of us is fighting her own battles with telling the truth:

> The heart is deceitful above all things
>   and beyond cure.
> Who can understand it? (Jeremiah 17:9)

> Do not lie to each other, since you have taken off your old self with its practices and have put on the new self, which is being renewed in knowledge in the image of its Creator. (Colossians 3:9-10)

> Therefore each of you must put off falsehood and speak truthfully to his neighbor, for we are all members of one body. (Ephesians 4:25)

Genuine Christians care deeply about truth, and most of us would never want to lie. But what if lying was so tricky and so clever that you indulged in it all the time without even knowing it? What if you found out that you were lying even when you thought you were the paragon of Christian virtue? What if, like many, you are falling into lying without even realizing it? Would you want to know?

This whole issue of the truth is a big one to our Lord. He even claims the word *truth* as one of his names (see John 14:6). Additionally he says that the only thing that can give us freedom is the truth (see John 8:32). Most of us know the basics of evangelical faith and don't waver on those too much. But I've found that lots of solid, Bible-believing people *do* have blind spots that keep them from seeing some of their thoughts and behaviors clearly. Could it be that a major reason for our lack of freedom and power in the Christian life is that we are largely unaware of these strongholds in ourselves?

WELCOME TO THE CLUB

The group I lead each week is composed of women and men who are struggling to change compulsive thoughts or behaviors in their lives. Some of them are compulsive about sex; some about getting everyone else's approval. Still others have problems with money, eating disorders or power struggles. One thing all of them have in common is relational masks.

As I finished teaching one night I opened the floor to questions and comments. Darrell immediately jumped in. "Russell, you failed to mention that 'Greater is he that is in me than he that is in the world.' Life is tough but I—and we—can do all things through him who strengthens us."

Darrell is a likable guy, but he is never forthright about what he feels. He overuses Bible verses or catchy phrases to solve every problem without ever dealing with it honestly. Darrell is a Spiritualizer.

Across the room I spotted Bill rolling his eyes. "Bill, is there something you'd like to say?" I asked. He jerked his head in surprise, unaware that I was watching.

"Oh, no," Bill replied. "I'm just listening." Bill did a lot of stuff like that. He also did it to his wife. She was so tired of his sleepwalking through life. He ate, watched TV and went to bed. The only way Bill would spring into action is if his pants were on fire. Bill is an Avoider.

"I think Bill *did* have something to say!" Margaret charged. Margaret is the Aggressor in the group. "Why can't you ever be honest, Bill? You sit here while other people pour out their guts, but you never take any risks. What's wrong with you!"

I affirmed Margaret's frustration, but I encouraged her to bring it down a notch. Thomas felt he needed to help me. "Whoa! No more coffee for *you,* sister!" he said with a grin. Then in a perfect Bill Clinton voice he said, "Can't we all just get along?" Everyone laughed (even Margaret), but this is how Thomas dealt with everything in life: with a joke. Thomas is a Deflector.

At this point Patty spoke up: "You guys can laugh all you want, but I think Bill needs to be understood. The few times he has spoken up you've made fun of him." She turned to face Bill and said with genuine warmth, "Bill, I think you're feeling a lot of pain. Could we pray for you?"

Bill shrugged with an if-you-want-to look on his face. I thanked Patty for her concern and reminded her that we would pray as a group momentarily. Patty was a wonderful woman, but she was always trying to "fix" people. Patty is a Savior.

The people in my group are very typical. They are a microcosm of the body of Christ and the world. You may have a boss who is an Aggressor: he constantly runs roughshod over your feelings and never sees your good points. You may be married to a Deflector: she jokes her way through life without really dealing with anything. She may also deflect her issues onto you when you attempt to confront her about something.

You may know a Self-Blamer: his self-image is so low that he brings a negative tone into everything he does. He is expert at cutting himself to ribbons but never doing anything to change (he is so "worthless" after all—why bother?). You probably know an Avoider: she frustrates you to no end because she will never lift a finger to grow or confront the tough stuff in her life.

You certainly know a Spiritualizer: he is holy, deep and wonderful. Some people are in awe of him (those who don't know him well). And others, who've seen him up close and personal, resent him for his hypocrisy and blindness. Spiritualizers know their Bible and have a ready answer for every problem. What they don't have is authenticity. You probably also know some Saviors: they are involved in ten different ministries and help every unfortunate soul they meet. Saviors have a God-given compassion, but they allow it to run amuck. They take care of everyone but themselves, to their own hurt.

Avoider, Aggressor, Deflector, Self-Blamer, Spiritualizer or Savior— any of these might be *you*.

So What's the Problem?

Everyone has idiosyncrasies, right? What's the problem if I'm a little pushy (like the Aggressor)? What's wrong with making people feel good and brightening this dismal world of ours (like the Deflector)? The problem is each of these relational masks is a perversion of a God-given strength. As we take a look in the pages ahead at these ways of interacting with each other, we will see that there are real problems with each one.

So many of us who hunger desperately to follow Jesus in all areas of our lives are tripping over our own feet. We may not smoke, drink or cuss, but these unresolved relating styles cause us to hurt the people around us. They keep us at a safe distance from God, and they cause us to fall into sins big and small if they aren't dealt with.

A great many of us have mastered the basic mindset and socially acceptable behaviors of a Christian, but we secretly wonder why there is no adventure in our relationship with God. We wonder why we aren't closer to the ones we love. And we wonder in the privacy of our hearts, *What's wrong with me? Why do I keep doing this?*

So many of us who hunger desperately to follow Jesus in all areas of our lives are tripping over our own feet.

You are about to meet Saviors, Self-Blamers, Avoiders, Deflectors, Aggressors and Spiritualizers. They are not evil people; they are broken people. You will see how the coping mechanisms they learned in childhood hardened into a way of relating to others as adults. You will see how and why this causes problems for them and those they relate to. And, most important, you will see how Jesus heals the person who is disordered in his very being.

STRONGHOLDS AND WORLDLY PATTERNS

As a new Christian in the seventies, I saw my share of strange teachings. One of them was on the subject of strongholds. Big-name evangelists would tell us that each geographical area had a unique satanic power base of lust or witchcraft. Our job, we were told, was to ask the Lord to identify the specifics of these strongholds and then to "pull them down."

We traveled to San Francisco or Washington to pray over the strongholds of homosexuality or liberal politics. We in the charismatic movement felt pretty important being on the inside track and having the goods on Satan. We believed that this insight enabled us to bring down his kingdom around his ears and, therefore, to advance the gospel. We based our teaching loosely on some texts in 2 Corinthians and Daniel. Missionaries instructed us further, based on information they had gathered from shamans and witch doctors from various Third World countries.

At special prayer meetings we would put on the whole armor of God, piece by piece, in elaborate rituals that guaranteed we'd be invincible against the devil. Yes, we were declaring all-out war on Satan! Unfortunately after church we were having affairs, mistreating our families or leading lives characterized by questionable ethics. The world was not impressed by our spirituality.

I don't believe we were mistaken about the importance of strongholds; I believe we were mistaken about what strongholds are. A close look at this biblical teaching shows that strongholds are not about demons at all; they are about *us*. Let me quote Paul and highlight the three things that he says strongholds are:

> The weapons we fight with are not the weapons of the world. On the contrary, they have divine power to demolish strongholds. We demolish *arguments* and every *pretension* that sets itself up against the knowledge of God, and we take captive every *thought* to make it obedient to Christ. (2 Corinthians 10:4-5, emphasis added)

Strongholds are not about demons at all; they are about *us*.

Arguments, pretensions, thoughts—these are the mental and emotional stuff of our daily struggles. Though Satan has a hand in their origin and maintenance, *we* are the primary caretakers of this fortress. Paul paints the picture of a mighty castle consisting of beliefs and relational masks that we've developed over a lifetime. Our loving God is trying (many times in vain) to move these walls out of the way. He persistently cries out to us, hoping we will help him take down the bricks. Our response determines how freely Jesus is allowed to interact with our hearts.

God's task—and ours—is made more difficult because many of us don't even see these strongholds. They are invisible to us, but a discerning person who gets to know us will be able to identify what they are. He could watch our behavior and monitor our emotions and get a pretty good fix on what our individual strongholds look like.

Paul tells us that these strongholds are the interior chalkboard on which the world writes its messages. He calls strongholds the "standards of this world" and says they are worldly wars and worldly weapons (2 Corinthians 10:2-4). That's why he says these worldly ideas and norms set themselves "up against the knowledge of God." They literally form a barrier against God's truth coming into our hearts.

In Romans 12:2 Paul says the same thing. He pleads with us not to "conform any longer to the pattern of this world." This "pattern of this world" is like the "standards of this world" in 2 Corinthians. Further he tells us to renew our minds. In other words, *we must change our beliefs*. If we attack the worldly beliefs still lurking in our hearts, we will be transformed, according to Paul. So you see, 2 Corinthians 10:2-4 and Romans 12:2 are complementary; they are saying the same thing.

What the Scriptures call strongholds, I am calling relational masks. If our relational masks form the walls, our core beliefs make up the bricks. Beliefs such as "If I am honest I will be abandoned" or "I must do everything perfectly or I am worthless" are the raw materials of our relational masks. To understand the Spiritualizer, the Deflector, the Savior, the Aggressor, the Self-Blamer and the Avoider, you will have to understand the beliefs that fuel them. That is the subject of our next chapter.

2

THE FOUNDATION OF RELATIONAL MASKS

Core Beliefs

Is it possible that many of us have beliefs deep inside that we don't even know about? If so, this would explain why there is such a difference between our stated beliefs and our lifestyles. It also makes sense that these core beliefs (whether true or false) would gradually shape our unique ways of relating to God and others. In looking at my own bitter struggles over the years, I have identified seven core beliefs that contribute to my relational masks. I have seen these same beliefs at work in the lives of countless other Christians.

CORE BELIEF #1: GOD CAN'T BE TRUSTED

Sherry was a wonderful Christian woman. Always dressed smartly, she was the epitome of confidence and self-assurance, but recently she had begun to feel depressed. She couldn't figure out why her husband, Will, and her kids always seemed mad at her. Increasingly they were accusing her of suffocating them and controlling their lives. She did her best to live the Christian life at home, but it seemed to make everyone resent her more. This didn't add up for her.

After a few sessions I felt comfortable enough to be direct with Sherry. "Your problem isn't with Will or the kids; it's with God. You don't believe God can be trusted."

Sherry was skeptical.

"Let's look at the facts: You say you trust God, but you are always fussing with the kids about one thing or another. You say you want Will to be the head of the house, but you are always telling him what to do. Your obsessive nagging is telling you something, Sherry."

She responded almost in slow motion. "I guess I really *don't* trust God." The room got very quiet. It always does when a stronghold becomes visible for the first time. Sherry's spirituality was being exposed, and she didn't like what she was seeing. But to her credit, she chose to be honest and not make excuses.

> **IF YOUR CORE BELIEF IS "GOD CAN'T BE TRUSTED" YOU WILL**
>
> • experience fear, panic and worry
>
> • shame yourself often about your lack of trust
>
> • get angry or depressed when things don't go your way
>
> • have a great need to control your life and the lives of others

Many of us learn this belief during our first fifteen years. It is our parents and other caregivers who model for us how to look at God. This might sound like psychobabble, but the Scriptures bear it out. God says, "You thought I was altogether *like you*" (Psalm 50:21, emphasis added). In another place he says, "God is not a man, that he should lie, nor a son of man, that he should change his mind. Does he speak and then not act? Does he promise and not fulfill?" (Numbers 23:19). In other words, he is not like our parents or others who've hurt us.

Many of us think that our view of God is shaped by Scripture alone, but if that is true, how do you explain our affairs, drug use, unloving treatment of others and struggles with fear and worry? Yes, it is sin in our lives, but it is also *pain* in our lives—pain that we have not had the honesty to look at or the courage to deal with.

Sherry manipulated every relationship in her life because she didn't really trust God to do the work. She learned this from a father who was out of town all the time and emotionally dead to her needs when he was home. She never felt truly loved or safe, though all her material needs were met. Because she felt she was "on her own" as a child, she continued operating that way as an adult. Thankfully she saw this and began dealing with it.

CORE BELIEF #2: THE BIBLE DOESN'T APPLY TO ME

I once asked a man why he didn't read his Bible. He began to tell me how busy he was at his shop. The cars rolled in all day long, he told me, and he was responsible to get them fixed. And when he got home he had the wife, the kids, the yard. Why, there just wasn't any time!

He also mentioned that the Bible was hard to understand. "If scholars can't figure it out after hundreds of years, then how can we?" he asked. His problem wasn't lack of time. He had time for the things that were important to him. His problem was that he didn't believe the Bible applied to him.

Not every Christian neglects his Bible; many take Scripture very seriously, but even someone who reads her Bible faithfully may still fall victim to this core belief. Cindy is a good example. Cindy led a Bible study that was attended by women from all over the city. She came to me because she had an anger problem. Though she was very sharp when it came to Scripture, she was not always a pleasant person to be around. "My husband also complains because I don't like sex," she said.

> **IF YOUR CORE BELIEF IS "THE BIBLE DOESN'T APPLY TO ME" YOU WILL**
>
> - read your Bible rarely or not at all
> - read and study diligently but not apply it
> - see whole sections of Scripture as irrelevant
> - delight in arguing theology but lack respect in your interactions with people
> - read lots of Christian books while your Bible gathers dust

Cindy told me she knew all about the "your body belongs to your husband" stuff. Though her husband was a kind man (by her admission) and never pushed the issue, she still resented him. Cindy resented a lot of things.

I began to wonder if her Bible knowledge was a cover for not feeling emotion. That was confirmed weeks later when she told me about being molested by her brother. Somewhere in her childhood she concluded that it did no good to feel. Feeling the pain didn't make the pain go away, and nobody cared about her feelings anyway. For her it was safer to bury her emotions and go after intellectual pursuits.

I showed her the rich biblical teaching about grieving your losses and feeling your feelings. Cindy admitted that she had never understood those verses and thought they were for "touchy-feely" types. She saw that refusing to feel emotions was very unbiblical, so she determined to *experience* her reality the way Scripture was freshly teaching her to do. She also realized that she needed a group of women who could minister to her. Being a lone ranger and ministering to everyone else was not enough.

CORE BELIEF #3: I DON'T NEED OTHER PEOPLE

Craig was a successful businessman. He came to me because his wife "made" him. When I asked him why, he told me a familiar story about how dissatisfied she was with their marriage and how she never stopped complaining. He told me his job required a lot of time, and when he was home he and his wife were little more than taxi drivers for their children's sporting events.

Craig's wife, Linda, gave me the other half of the story: Craig positioned himself in front of the TV each night and spent every weekend hitting golf balls. Craig admitted that this was true but defended himself. "Can't a man relax?" he asked with annoyed frustration.

"Craig, what your actions are telling me is that you don't need other people."

"Of course I need other people," he protested.

"For what?" I asked.

Craig just stared at me for the longest time. I allowed my question to hang in the air without uttering another word. Finally he said something about wanting love and companionship "same as everyone else." Again I pointed out that his actions demonstrated something different. It was a remote or a golf club that he really sought companionship with.

"I guess something is wrong with that picture, huh?" he half asked, half stated.

This is where many of us live. We rush from one task to another, busying ourselves with housework, yard work or "serving the Lord," all the while neglecting the relationships closest to us. We build a life that is as self-sufficient as we are able to make it. Of course, nobody really succeeds at this, but it gives us the illusion of autonomy.

UNDERCUTTING THE FOUNDATION

Whether we avoid closeness with others through busyness or through isolation, these behaviors attack the very foundation of Christianity. Jesus said the entire Old Testament hangs on two commands: Love God and love the person next to you (Matthew 22:34-40). How can you love the person next to you and not open

Whether we avoid closeness with others through busyness or through isolation, these behaviors attack the very foundation of Christianity.

your heart to him? And how can you open your heart without letting yourself be vulnerable? Peter wrote, "Above all, love each other deeply" (1 Peter 4:8). Above all ministry, business obligations, "Christian" stuff and evangelistic enterprises, we are to deeply, vulnerably love those next to us.

Obviously there are people with whom it isn't safe to open our hearts. This is to be expected. The writers of Scripture knew we couldn't get along with *everyone* (see Romans 12:18). They also knew there would be people who would hurt and wound us, hence, the need to be careful (Matthew 7:6; 10:17; John 2:24-25; 2 Thessalonians 3:2). But statements like these do not relieve us of the need to take relational risks.

Are you risking? Is there someone who really knows you—someone to whom you show your tender underbelly? Do the things you share with a close friend occasionally terrify you? If you answer no to these questions, you are living under the illusion that you really don't need others. At least you don't need them in any way that counts.

And it won't do to say, "There isn't anybody I trust." What that really means is you've chosen not to be honest with anybody until it is completely safe. Is that the Christian life? Choosing all your words with utmost care so that nobody ever sees inside? That's the way the *world* lives.

While on earth, our Lord didn't have a problem admitting his need for

IF YOUR CORE BELIEF IS "I DON'T NEED OTHER PEOPLE" YOU WILL

- be offended every time someone points out one of your faults

- be superficial in most of your relationships

- never reveal anything about yourself that could get you into trouble

- interact with Christians only around activities or theological discussions but never cut to the heart

- rarely, if ever, ask anyone for help

- feel guilty and weak when you do have to ask for help

human support and emotional help (see Matthew 26:38). But we have a problem with this because sin tricks us into thinking we are supposed to stand without assistance. Thankfully the small-group movement around the world is dispelling this arrogant lie. Actually this movement has merely called us back to a vulnerable interdependence that the writers of Scripture always preached.

Seeing the importance of this, I began meeting weekly with a friend of mine. I was already involved in church, small-group meetings and individual therapy, but I felt the real goal was to have a true brother with whom I could be totally honest. It started as an accountability thing, but we sensed that God was trying to create something deeper.

After eighteen months I had a strange experience as we sat together in a restaurant. I felt a surge of emotion rising up in my heart. It was a mixture of affection and gratitude. It scared me. Was our friendship crossing some forbidden boundary? Was this a sign of homosexuality? I didn't know, but I took a risk. "Brian, I love you"—my throat caught on the words—"and I need your friendship."

> **Sin tricks us into thinking we are supposed to stand without assistance.**

Brian smiled and told me that he appreciated my taking that risk. That was almost ten years ago. We are two men thankful to have a brother in the world. Our relationship has also helped us love our wives and kids better because we routinely confront the selfishness in each other.

CORE BELIEF #4: INTIMATE RELATIONSHIPS BRING ONLY PAIN

Those who practice the "I don't need others" lifestyle are actually dealing with a second core belief. Their disconnection or superficial relating shows that they are trying to live without being honestly dependent on others, but why are they doing this? What is the core belief beneath the core belief? It is this: Intimate relationships bring only pain.

A pastor I know is a good example of this. He's on a dozen committees and has started or assisted in scores of ministries over the years. Literally thousands have come to Christ through his preaching, and God has definitely used him in a powerful way. Here's the problem: he has failed in important relationships in his life.

He has battled infidelity. Many who've been on his staff have been insulted, demeaned or abused by his exercise of "authority." Those who question him or dare to disagree have been told directly that they aren't hearing from God. How do you explain a man like this? He is evangelical and he is social, but he is not *relational*.

A MAN CALLED PETER

Does Scripture give any examples of this? It does, and his name is Peter. We get a hint of Peter's fear of intimacy in chapter five of Luke. He seems outwardly cordial when Jesus suggests that he let down the nets for another catch. Then suddenly the nets fill up. Peter sees that a miracle is happening and responds in a very strange way: "Go away from me, Lord; I am a sinful man!" (Luke 5:8).

Why was Peter so panicky to get away from Jesus? Apart from the sheer weight of Jesus' holiness and supernatural power, Peter was fighting with something else. He was fighting with an inner voice: *Oh, no! He knows what I'm really like!* He was afraid of being known. But instead of leaving, the man with the piercing eyes said, "Don't be afraid; from now on you will catch men" (Luke 5:10).

Over the next few years Peter saw miracle after miracle. Still he continued to be afraid in this part of his heart. During dinner one evening Jesus said something like this: "Peter, in spite of your perceived loyalty and allegiance, your fragile ego will collapse tonight and you will betray me." Peter *knew* he was incapable of such a thing. In reality he was not intimate enough with his own heart to know how treacherous it really was.

Those who fear intimacy with others do so because they are not intimate with the deeper issues of their own hearts. They know themselves to a point, but their deeper fears are hidden from them. When Jesus tries to point these out to us, our response is predictable: "No, Lord, that isn't true of me. You know I would never do such a thing!"

This is why so many Christians struggle with pornography, eating disorders and a host of other unmanageable behaviors. They are afraid of the pain they anticipate from intimate relationships. Yet because they were made for such relationships they cannot kill the desire completely. So they seek out a substitute.

Jesus gave Peter another opportunity to see what was in his heart. He asked repeatedly if Peter loved him (John 21:15-22). Basically he was saying, "Peter, we went over this a few weeks ago and you didn't want to look at it. So let's try again: Do you really love me as much as you think, or is your love actually shallow?" There is only one honest answer: "Lord, you are right. I'm not half as spiritual as I'd like to think. Please help me to become real." When God asks a question, it's always an invitation, like his plaintive call to Adam to admit that he was hiding from something. Jesus told Peter,

IF YOUR CORE BELIEF IS "INTIMATE RELATIONSHIPS BRING ONLY PAIN" YOU WILL

- be friendly and social but nobody will really know you
- be addicted to work, hobbies, committees or ministries
- talk in clichés but never reveal your soul
- feel panic whenever emotions of loneliness or fear rise up
- almost never take risks in your relationships

"Feed my sheep" and "follow me." In other words, "Get close to me, get close to my people and care for their needs." He was commanding Peter to be relational.

Those who fear intimacy with others do so because they are not intimate with the deeper issues of their own hearts.

When we discover the truth about ourselves, we find that it is as bad as we feared (in fact, it's worse). But only *then* does this incredible grace of his really hit the spot. When you are touched by that kind of love a few hundred times, you lose your fear of someone else finding you out, because the One who really matters has already found you out, and you are okay with him. This must begin before we can truly move toward intimacy with others.

CORE BELIEF #5: ROMANCE OR SEX WILL MEET MY DEEPEST NEEDS

Carl was a successful missionary. He and his wife, Sally, were enjoying a much-needed furlough in the mountains of central California. One morning Sally sat down in front of the computer. As she tapped the mouse, something appeared on the screen—and it took her breath away. In front of her was the most shocking pornographic image she'd ever seen. For a moment she just stared.

Sally called her husband over. "Do you know where *this* came from?" she asked.

When Carl stepped around to see the screen, his eyes got wide and he swallowed hard. "No," he said unconvincingly, "someone must have e-mailed it by mistake."

Sally didn't buy it. At first Carl denied everything, but after an hour of interrogation and threats it all came out. He admitted he had a porn problem and, not only that, many of his female "coworkers" in Brazil had been more than friends. Sally's perfect Christian world ended that day. That's when they came to me.

"How could a man of God fall into this?" they wondered aloud. Didn't Carl teach the Bible all over South America? Hadn't dozens of churches been planted that were sending out missionaries of their own? How could these two worlds coexist in the same man?

A family history revealed that Carl was raised by missionary parents himself. They left him with relatives and various boarding schools while they served the Lord as they thought best. When they were together as a family, they were functional but not close. This created a huge vacuum in Carl's heart that pushed him toward pornography at age eight. Later he moved on to cyber-porn and secret affairs in adulthood. Carl believed that sex would meet his deepest needs.

A ONE-WOMAN MAN

Matthew was different from Carl. He didn't use pornography or masturbation to meet his needs. He used his wife Kim.

"Matt is *obsessed* with sex," Kim told me. "Sure, it was great when we first got married, but after twelve years he still isn't satisfied and he won't stop bugging me about it."

Matthew was embarrassed by her statement. "There's nothing wrong with being attracted to your wife," he said. "There are women out there who *wish* their husbands were interested in them."

Over the next few weeks I found out that—contrary to what Matt said—Kim enjoyed sex. On average they made love two to three times a week, but once in a great while they would go eight or ten days without. During those occasions Matthew would yell, call Kim the most vicious names and punch holes in the wall.

Matthew didn't know it, but he came into marriage believing that sex and romance would meet all his needs. He was certainly a one-woman man, but woe to that woman if she didn't meet his expectations. I asked Matt about his relationship with his children.

"Well, I believe in lots of hugs, kisses and words of affection," he said.

"That seems real important to you as a father."

"It is, because my mom never . . ." His eyes began to moisten.

"Because your mom never what?" I asked.

"Because my mom never showed affection that way."

"Maybe that was more important than you've wanted to admit," I suggested.

Matthew's mom was married to housework. She never really touched him or his soul. From childhood on, an unmet desire for nurture followed him wherever he went. By the time he met Kim he was almost crazy with the thought, *I will have a woman who loves me.* Kim didn't stand a chance.

The idea that sex or romance will meet all, or most, of our emotional needs is something I call "romantic orthodoxy." Romantic orthodoxy is preached in almost every love song, romance novel and romantic comedy. A crude version is preached in pornography. Christians couch romantic orthodoxy differently in their conferences and books: Follow such and such principles, be a good spouse, and your husband or wife will meet all your needs.

Now, before you assume that I'm

IF YOUR CORE BELIEF IS "ROMANCE OR SEX WILL MEET MY DEEPEST NEEDS" YOU WILL

- feel lots of anger toward your spouse
- only feel loved if you are being romantic or sexual
- work really hard to change your spouse
- use pornography, be hooked on romance novels or be unfaithful
- fight with incredible loneliness
- believe (as a single) that most of your problems will be solved by marriage

just a bitter old married person, understand where I'm coming from. I've been married to my first and last sweetheart for more than twenty years. I can honestly say that we are still in love and that sex is good (sometimes great!). But it took years of disillusionment and pain before my romantic orthodoxy finally died and I was able to accept the reality that marriage is not a cure-all. The truth is this: the Bible nowhere promises unbroken bliss to married Christians.

BUT WHAT ABOUT . . . ?

But doesn't the Bible celebrate romantic love? Isn't there a whole book devoted to the joys of married sex (Song of Songs)? Isn't "the way of a man with a maiden" amazing (Proverbs 30:18-19)? Yes, Scripture includes all of this and more, but let's be clear about what the Bible *doesn't* say: it doesn't say that romance or sex will meet all our needs.

Again, most Christians would be quick to agree, but a look at their lives, relationships and emotional struggles reveals a different set of beliefs. Like Matthew and Carl, many men believe that the perfect woman (or women) will satisfy their soul's hunger. Their addiction to pornography, constant rubbernecking or repeated affairs bears this out. For men this issue is so complex that I've written an entire book on the subject.[1] Regardless of what our culture or hormones tell us, the perfect woman will not meet our deepest needs.

Yet we persist in this belief. For instance, when we look at the sage advice in Ephesians 5, this is what it sounds like to many women: "Wives, submit to your husbands as to the Lord *and then they will treat you like queens, meeting all of your emotional needs.*" This is what the men read: "Husbands, love your wives, just as Christ loved the church; *then they will be so smitten by you that they'll overwhelm you in bed every night.*"

There are at least three agendas at work in every marriage: the husband's, the wife's and God's. When men are honest, many admit that they look to marriage to provide unlimited sexual access, a comfortable home and a degree of companionship. And many women look to marriage to provide unlimited financial and emotional security.

Our romantic and domestic needs matter to God, but they are not his primary interest. In marriage God puts two people in a relationship that pushes all their unspoken beliefs and longings to the surface. This is the only way these can be seen and dealt with. Disappointments and struggles are what God uses to conform many of us to "the likeness of his Son" (Romans 8:29). It is a very effective crucible. Sadly, half of all married Christians fail to understand this, and they jump ship.

> **Disappointments and struggles are what God uses to conform many of us to "the likeness of his Son."**

So, Christian husband, love your wife and be sacrificially kind to her, but don't make the mistake of thinking she'll meet all your needs. Christian wife, be affectionate and caring of this man, but don't expect him to fill your emotional void. Christian, whether single and divorced, affirm the value of marriage, but don't believe the lies that marriage will heal all your wounds. There is only one who can satisfy to that depth, and he says, "If anyone is thirsty, let him [or her] come to *me* and drink" (John 7:37, emphasis added).

CORE BELIEF #6: I MUST DO EVERYTHING PERFECTLY OR I AM WORTHLESS

Joan came to me after I had worked with her husband for a while. Tim had grown rapidly, but she still wasn't happy. She thought she *would* be when he got "fixed," but as he got more healthy, her soul sickness became more obvious. The two of them met with me to discuss their relationship.

"Joan is the most capable person I know," Tim said. "When something needs to get done, she's the woman for the job but . . ."

"But what?" I asked.

"Well, I don't want to make her feel bad, but she's downright neurotic."

They both stifled a nervous laugh. I asked Joan what Tim was talking about.

"I *am* a perfectionist," she said. "I seem to have a hard time with anything that doesn't come out just right."

When I asked for examples, they told me stories about fights with each other, fights with their kids and disagreements over "what the neighbors will think." It seemed Joan couldn't let anybody make mistakes or perceive her family as flawed. This had its beginnings in the way her family operated when she was a child.

When Joan was little, her mom literally controlled everything she did or said. Not surprisingly, Joan attempted to manage everyone and everything in her own life when she became an adult. She was already shaming her five-year-old daughter for things that were perfectly normal for a child. Yet she had sworn to herself that she'd never do that to her kids. As good-hearted as Joan was, she harbored a tremendous fear: eventually others will find out how imperfect I am and reject me.

IF YOUR CORE BELIEF IS "I MUST DO EVERYTHING PERFECTLY OR I AM WORTHLESS" YOU WILL

- be obsessed with cleanliness, order and perfection
- be very angry and depressed whenever you make a mistake or fail at something
- judge others or yourself with an impossible standard
- have a very rigid or legalistic Christianity
- fight constant battles over your self-worth

THE POWER OF SHAME

Next to God, shame is one of the most powerful forces in the universe. It all started with our original great-grandparents. Prior to their disastrous Fall, Adam and Eve enjoyed a total lack of shame. They had no fear of God, each other or the world around them. The Scriptures say they were naked yet felt no shame (Genesis 2:25). This doesn't mean simply that they were nude; it means that they were completely free with each other. When they sinned, this inner freedom and contentment were snuffed out. This death affected them at every level of their being and was passed on to us.

> **Jesus didn't come only to forgive**
> **our sin and make us productive citizens.**
> **He came to set us free.**

Good evangelistic preaching has always emphasized how the cross cancels sin, reverses the curse and secures heaven for us. This is absolutely true, but we don't take it far enough. Jesus didn't come only to forgive our sin and make us productive citizens. He came to set us free from this centuries-old bondage. How rare the Christian who has tasted this!

Do not be afraid; you will not suffer shame.
  Do not fear disgrace; you will not be humiliated.
You will forget the shame of your youth
  and remember no more the reproach of your widowhood.
(Isaiah 54:4)

Why does God tell us this? Because we *do* fear shame and disgrace. This fear is the driving force behind much of what we do and what we show to the world. Most of us—even Christians—live our lives hiding and protecting our fragile souls, because the liberation of God has not reached us at this level. This hinders everything from our prayer life to our sex life.

Imagine what we'd be like if we could be even partially free from this tormenting fear. How would we interact with our spouse? What would we do when someone caught us in a mistake? How would we react to the judgments and criticism of others? How would we worship? All of these would be very different if God took away our shame, and that is exactly what he wants to do.

CORE BELIEF # 7: IF I AM HONEST I WILL BE ABANDONED

During one of our stays at my grandparents' house, I was sitting at the table drawing a picture. As a ten-year-old there was nothing I loved better than drawing. My grandpa was home and, thanks to a six-pack of beer, was in a pretty foul mood. My family is notoriously racist, so I wasn't surprised when my grandpa said, "This house is a mess. It looks like a bunch of Mexicans live here!" Why Mexicans or blacks or whatever were synonymous with dirt I never understood. To prove that, I said, "What's wrong with Mexicans, Grandpa? They're people too."

I wasn't trying to be a smart aleck; it just seemed like common sense to me. That's why I was surprised—and terrified—when he took a quick step toward my chair and kicked it as hard as he could. The top of his foot caught it just beneath my butt. The chair jerked violently up into the air and seemed to hang there for a second and then came down again on all fours.

I wasn't hurt—at least not physically—but I felt very afraid. He stood there for a moment, his face twitching in anger. I didn't know what was going to happen next. Thankfully he regained his composure and walked out of the room without a word. To be assaulted like this by a family member is rejection itself. I was reminded that day of a lesson I would learn many times in my family: if I am honest I will be abandoned.

HELD IN SLAVERY

All of us have learned, in one form or another, that lying is the best way to keep people on our side. How else do you explain our routine deceitfulness?

- A friend asks, "How are you?" and you say, "Fine," even if depression is clawing out your insides.

- Your husband says, "Is something wrong, honey?" and you say, "No," even though you're mad enough to tear his head off.

- As you pray, you are racked with fear or doubt but say something "spiritual" to God instead of what you're really feeling.

- You are confronted about something you did but have an irrational fear of admitting that the other person is right. So you justify yourself or point out what *he* did wrong.

These are just a few examples of the way we dodge truth. In fact we are so accustomed to it that any other lifestyle seems nearly impossible to us. Many of us learned this from a hundred teachers and ten thousand reinforcements.

This is not a new problem. On one occasion the Lord told the Pharisees exactly what he thought of their rules. When he did this, the disciples took him aside and said, "Do you know that the Pharisees were offended when they heard this?" (Matthew 15:12).

Didn't Jesus know that you don't say things like that in polite society? Our Master knew *exactly* what he was doing, and he knew exactly what would happen to him as a result. We, too, have an innate sense of what could happen to us if we are truly honest. If we aren't killed (like our Master), we will certainly be humiliated or looked down on, we fear. What death is to the body, abandonment is to the soul.

We fear this abandonment deeply. In Hebrews we are told that our Lord died to free us who "all [our] lives were held in slavery by [our] fear of death" (Hebrews 2:14-15). But it isn't just the death of our body we fear. We also fear the death of our identity and value. Many of us—even Christians—are held in slavery to our fear. Even the person who prides herself in not caring what anybody thinks is bound by it. That's why she insults people before they can do it to her.

> **IF YOUR CORE BELIEF IS "IF I AM HONEST I WILL BE ABANDONED" YOU WILL**
>
> - be friendly and nice but not candid
> - blend in with whatever group or person you are with
> - not dare to have an unpopular opinion
> - believe that arguments or disagreements are always bad
> - use lots of "God-talk" in prayer but never bare your soul

In Psalm 15 we are told what kind of person dwells in God's sanctuary and lives on his "holy hill": the one "who does what is righteous, *who speaks the truth from his heart*" (Psalm 15:2, emphasis added). Speaking the truth from your heart doesn't mean you say flowery things about Jesus. It means you express with your mouth what you are really feeling inside—no matter how unnerving it may be to others. Yes, you must consider the people around you, but don't confuse "being loving" with being dishonest.

God is not telling us that we must be honest in order to be righteous. He's telling us that we must be honest in order to be intimate. Intimacy is something everyone wants (though we settle for many counterfeits). But unless we walk in the light of honesty we cannot have intimacy with God or others (see 1 John 1:5-7). This is absolutely key to the entire Christian faith. Yet how many of us will tell a dozen "white lies" before the day is over?

My wife and I experienced the paradox of fear and intimacy on a recent trip to the California coast. We had worked hard to arrange childcare, finances and a dozen other details so that we could get away and relax. After the movies, dinners out and running around town, we finally had a chance to sit by the beach and watch the waves.

For several days I had had a restless "something" going on inside my heart, but I didn't want to tell my wife on our nineteenth anniversary that I was bored with our marriage. As we sat side by side and wordlessly watched the ocean, Keri turned to me. "I don't know how to say this," she said, "but it's been bugging me for days, so I guess I'll just have to come out with it: I don't like where our relationship is. I . . . I feel like we're in a dead place." She couldn't speak anymore because she was crying.

I was stunned. Not because my feelings were hurt but because she took the words right out of my mouth. I knew the Lord was in it. He wasn't in our deadness, but he was in its exposure. Here we were, two people busy with kids and jobs, feeling restless about a love affair gone cold. And Jesus didn't want us to stay there. But somebody had to say something. That somebody was my wife. As she choked on her words, I told her she didn't have to be afraid. I told her I was feeling the same thing and God wanted us to be honest with each other about it.

It was really weird. We sat there holding hands, admitting our mutual deadness—and feeling closer than we ever had before. We decided to recommit ourselves to being truly intimate with each other and to making that a priority in spite of the ongoing pressures of our lives. It's true: you cannot have fellowship unless you walk in the light.

CONCLUSION

These core beliefs dictate many of our thoughts, feelings and behaviors, but often we don't know this because the beliefs are outside our conscious awareness. Our Lord wants to demolish them so we can have freedom and joy. But there is one more problem: these core beliefs have seeped into the fabric of our personalities. This has shaped how we relate to God, ourselves and others. It's time now to take a close look at each relational mask.

3

THE AVOIDER

Smoldering Rebel

Frank was a lonely child. His father wasn't involved in his life in any meaningful way, and whenever Frank's parents had a conflict in their marriage, his dad simply shut down and refused to speak. This was the model Frank had. He hated his father's emotional deadness and resented the lack of closeness between them. But he dealt with this feeling of abandonment by hiding in a world of books, music and isolation.

When Frank grew up, he married Evelyn, his college sweetheart. Things started going downhill pretty fast. He began soliciting prostitutes. When Evelyn found out, it just about destroyed their marriage. But Frank made good on his promise to change. What persisted, however, was a problem almost as big: passivity. Evelyn told me she couldn't stand the passive-aggressive stuff anymore.

When they first came to see me, Frank said he would do "anything" to save the marriage. He then entered one of our groups and did individual counseling as well. Unfortunately he would come to the group and say almost nothing to the men. They would ask him questions and he would say, "I don't know," with a shrug. He shared about his thoughts or feelings only if it was dragged out of him. The guys in the group were very frustrated with him.

In counseling he and I weren't doing much better. When I asked him what was going on, he gave me a shrug as well. When we did decide on a given course of action (Bible study, accountability and so on), he would never follow through. Evelyn would get angry and hurt by his passivity and threaten to move out or have him move. At those times he would always rally and say he was ready to "deal with things," but it never lasted long. Frank was an Avoider.

It all came to a head one day when Evelyn asked him to help with a family task. Frank agreed, but he let hours go by without doing a thing. When she mentioned it again, he blew up. She responded by telling him that she was fed up with his adultery, laziness and passivity. If this was how it was going to be, she said, she was through.

He reacted by walking out the door without a word. Evelyn didn't hear from him for a day and a half. When he did call he was drunk and in a motel room. He told her that he'd been with a hooker all night and that he was sorry. He would do anything to make it right, he said. She said she wouldn't even talk to him unless I was present.

When the three of us sat together, I asked him what he was going to do about this. He gave a vague answer about seeking the Lord and trying harder. When I asked him what that meant, he couldn't tell me. Evelyn was fuming. I could tell she was on the verge of calling it quits (and I wouldn't have blamed her), but, to her credit, she said she would give him one more opportunity to deal with his avoidance. As heinous as the sexual immorality was, it was his avoidant personality that fueled it.

Over the next few weeks I met with Frank and Evelyn separately. I told Frank that his marriage was hanging by a thread. He said lots of things, but he didn't seem willing to take any real action. I knew the clock was ticking. When I met with Evelyn I told her she had every right to divorce her husband, but I pleaded with her to extend grace. I knew how difficult it was to deal with an avoidant person, I told her. *I* had been one since childhood. But I asked her to consider

God's heart for reconciliation.

I was amazed that Frank didn't grasp the severity of the situation. He seemed to think this would soon blow over, and his wife would get off his back. When that didn't happen, he got angry. During a fight he threw a punch bowl against the wall and shattered it. Evelyn stood there expressionless and calmly said, "Frank, I'm through." He packed his things with a sorrowful face as though he'd been unjustly treated. He moved into a motel room and waited for Evelyn to come around. She didn't. She was serious this time. She had given him countless second chances, but his years of blame, anger and infidelity had finally killed what was left in the heart of this once gentle woman.

> **YOU MIGHT BE AN AVOIDER IF**
> - you procrastinate a lot or fail to finish the things you start
> - you get along with everybody and never make waves
> - what matters to you most is peace and tranquility
> - people in your life are always accusing you of avoiding things
> - you avoid those people

When Frank came for counseling again, there was a desperation I'd never seen. I think he was finally serious, but Evelyn wasn't budging this time. His lifelong foot dragging had finally cost him his marriage and his children. His wife, countless men and the Holy Spirit had pleaded with him for years to end his stonewalling behavior. He had steadfastly refused. When he realized that he really had burned the bridge, he drove his car to a vineyard and ran a vacuum hose from the tailpipe to the driver's window. When a farm worker found him slumped over in the front seat, Frank was in a coma. He remains in a coma to this day.

A MAN WHO REMAINS

The Scriptures make a chilling prophecy about the Avoider: "A man who remains stiff-necked after many rebukes will suddenly be destroyed—without remedy" (Proverbs 29:1). When the Avoider persists in her avoidant, evasive behavior, she becomes the agent of her own destruction. Most Avoiders will not end up like Frank, but they will pay a price. And it will be heavy if they don't repent.

Every Avoider believes he just can't help the way he is. Avoiding the difficult issues of life makes things really hard, but the Avoider believes that *dealing* with things would be even harder. Many Avoiders come into old age with deep regrets. As old men or women they realize they could have done things differently, hindsight being what it is. By that time they can only lament the lost opportunities, the shattered families and the unfulfilled dreams.

Every Avoider believes he just can't help the way he is.

Men and women who adopt this relational mask find that by their twenties they are pretty locked in. I know. This is how I chose to deal with the pain in my own family. When my father left and my mother turned to drink and revolving relationships, I started giving in to my hopelessness. Prior to that I had tried for years to make the best of things and influence the crazy behavior of the adults around me, but to no avail. I began to retreat into a world of reading and drawing— a fantasy world.

When I was a child, this actually kept me sane. God allowed me to "check out" so I wouldn't be further damaged by the madness all around me. But a strange thing happened on the way to adulthood. I got saved. At sixteen I finally found someone who would love me and care for me, and his name was Jesus. I was deliriously happy for a while. It wasn't long, however, before the Lord began to deal with my escapist approach to life. I didn't like it one bit. Hadn't I been through enough already? I thought becoming a Christian would bring some comfort and peace. Without realizing it, I was using my Christianity as a tool of avoidance as well.

What God did in my life (and continues to do) was send person after person to confront my passivity and self-pity. He used bosses, pastors, friends and enemies to rattle my cage. I almost always directed my anger at the messenger. I quit jobs, ended relationships and felt pretty justified in my rage at life's unfairness—but Jesus wasn't buying it. When I got away from one "troublesome" person, he saw to it that I bumped into another. Finally I started to realize that he wasn't letting me off the hook.

Oh, the pity-parties I threw! "Nobody *else* has to put up with this!" I would rant at God. "Don't worry about them," he'd always say. "Do you want to follow me or not?" In spite of my frustration as a professional martyr, I did want to obey him. So I let him rebuild my personality, tearing it down one brick at a time and replacing each brick with another. Dealing with this has been the hardest thing I've ever done. It's been harder than overcoming my sexual addiction, weight problem and childhood abuse combined. But cooperating with God in this process is giving me more freedom than I ever thought possible.

A MAN AFTER GOD

David is my Old Testament hero for many reasons. Warrior, prophet, king—he had it all. The main reason I love him is that he knew how desperately he needed God and wasn't afraid to admit it.

But David had a hidden personality flaw: he was an Avoider. When it came to battles and worship services, he was passionate and fierce (as many Avoiders are on the job or athletic field), but in his closest relationships he was downright listless. Before David came to the throne, this didn't seem to be a problem, but shortly after he became king, this hidden defect began to rise to the surface.

It shows itself early in David's relationships. David had two men on his staff who were Aggressors (more on that in chapter seven). Joab and his brother Abishai were ruthless men who would stop at nothing to fulfill their agendas. When they didn't like a man, they had no problem setting a trap for him or killing him in cold blood (2 Samuel 3:22-30; 16:5-10; 18:10-14; 20:8-12). Not only did David fail to deal with these two, he also passed the buck to his son to take care of later (1 Kings 2:5-6).

Where this is recounted in Scripture, we read something interesting: "In the spring, at the time when kings go off to war, *David sent Joab*" (2 Samuel 11:1, emphasis added). David was willing to keep Joab around (ruthless as he was) because he could use Joab to accomplish his dirty work. With Joab off fighting the king's battles, what was a bored monarch to do? He found a cutie next door and decided to have sex with her. When Bathsheba turned up pregnant, David needed her husband to disappear, so once again he called on his faithful sidekick Joab to get the job done (2 Samuel 11:14-27).

> **THINGS AVOIDERS SAY:**
>
> "What's the big deal? I'll get around to it!"
>
> "I don't want to talk about that right now."
>
> "That's all in the past."
>
> "I can't do that."
>
> "I can't help it."
>
> "It will take too long."
>
> "God understands my weakness."
>
> Nothing.

In my work with sexually addicted men, I have found one trait common to all of them: passivity. They may be killers in the boardroom, construction site or baseball diamond, but in their closest relationships they are passive and weak. Many of them use sex to make themselves feel better. This is exactly what happened to David when he was avoiding his responsibilities.

Not only do Avoiders hurt their spouse and use the people closest to them, they always hurt their kids too. When Tamar (David's daughter) was sexually abused by her stepbrother Amnon, the king was furious but *did* nothing (2 Samuel 13:1-21). When his son Absalom found out about Tamar's rape, he told her, "Be quiet now, my sister; he is your brother. Don't take this thing to heart" (2 Samuel 13:20). Avoidance had become a family trait.

When Absalom did take action, because his father wouldn't, he ended up killing Amnon and fleeing the country. During the three years when Absalom was gone, David ached to be with him but, once again, did nothing (2 Samuel 13:37-39). When David the Avoider wouldn't do anything to restore his relationship with Absalom, Joab the Aggressor did. This is typical. Where you find an Avoider you often find an Aggressor doing everything the Avoider refuses to do.

Joab arranged to have Absalom brought back, but David refused to meet with his son face-to-face. This avoidance frustrated Absalom so deeply that he set a field on fire to get the attention he wanted (2 Samuel 14:23-33). Absalom finally saw his father, but their relationship didn't improve. By that time David's lifelong career as an Avoider had embittered Absalom completely. Absalom's feelings of rejection turned to rage, and he began trying to manipulate his way onto the throne. This conspiracy grew into a civil war that eventually claimed twenty thousand lives—including Absalom's.

Where you find an Avoider you often find an Aggressor doing everything the Avoider refuses to do.

What point am I making? It is this: all the people around David made their own choices, but David's life as an Avoider had a *huge* impact on them. Death and destruction were the result. Whether you are a father of two or a mother of four, if you are an Avoider, your spouse, friends and children will be negatively affected before it's all over. Yet this is one hundred percent avoidable.

BUCKLE UP

What can the Avoider do to change something that seems so innate? I had this discussion with Cynthia. Cynthia is a forty-six-year-old woman who feels as though her life has been pointless. She married young in hopes that her husband would give her life meaning. He didn't. In fact he quickly grew tired of her dull and monotonous approach to life. He found someone who would take some risks and ran off with her, leaving Cynthia with two children. She poured herself into her kids and admits that she "spoiled" them (interpretation: lots of syrupy love but few boundaries and little direction).

Ironically her kids grew up to feel very *unloved* because she never exercised consistent discipline, though she would yell and lose her composure when they didn't appreciate "all she did." Cynthia was hurt by key people in her life, including her husband and her children. Somewhere along the line she decided to stop engaging life. This decision, reinforced thousands of times over the years, grew into her way of relating to the world. She came to me because she was starting to see that life was passing her by. At forty-six, it was half over.

"As I look back I see so many things that I could have done differently," she told me. When I asked her what those were, she mentioned marrying a man who she knew at the time was not fit to be a husband. I asked her if anyone had pointed his unfitness out to her. She said yes, they had, but she hadn't listened. When she had an opportunity to go to night school and learn a skill, she didn't. She was too afraid of failure, she told me. When she began having problems with her children, she didn't get counseling, read any books or pursue any kind of help. Life was just too busy, she said.

We talked about opportunity after opportunity that she had passed up. How she wished she had taken some risks and tried some things, she lamented.

"How about now?" I asked.

"What do you mean?"

"You said there were many opportunities you could have taken, but you didn't. Are you letting opportunities pass you by today?"

Cynthia didn't want to go in this direction, but I pressed the point. "Cynthia, you're telling me that half your life has been wasted. Obviously there's nothing you can do about that now, but what will you do with the second half?"

She grew noticeably uncomfortable, but to her credit she brought her pounding heart back into the conversation. I suggested that maybe she had experienced failure in the past, but this was a new day. Was she going to hide behind her "this is just how I am" persona or was she ready to do things differently? She took a deep breath as if to gather strength and said, "I'm ready to make a change."

> **THINGS AVOIDERS DO:**
> - pass the buck
> - drag their feet
> - believe that everyone is out to get them
> - excel in their strengths and refuse to grow in areas of weakness
> - rarely connect with God
> - infuriate those around them
> - nothing

Over the next few months we worked on Cynthia's core beliefs. Her top two were "Intimacy only brings pain" and "I have to be perfect or I am worthless." Her core beliefs had kept her from letting anyone into her life in any meaningful way and from trying anything that carried with it the possibility of failure. She had developed a relational mask that kept everyone out of her dull and predictable world. She had gone to church, but she arrived late and left early. She was very conservative in her views and told herself this was "Christian." Anything that aroused excitement or hope in her was immediately pushed out of her heart.

Cynthia had become very cold toward God as well. Sporadic church attendance and watching Christian television was the extent of her spirituality. She knew she "should" read her Bible and do a lot of other things, but she never did. I told her it was time to join the human race and engage what she had left of life. The old fears attacked her mercilessly, but she was determined not to be cheated out of living anymore.

We agreed that the first thing she needed to do was find a church where she would be fed. This removed her excuse of avoiding church because it was "so boring." I told her to visit five churches and ask the Lord to reveal where he wanted her. At first she was resistant and said something about "church hoppers." I pointed out that someone who had been at a church for twenty-two years could hardly call herself a church hopper.

With great fear and trembling she visited each church and found one where the pastor seemed to be "reading her mail" every Sunday morning. She began growing quickly. I told her to find a women's group to attend. When she did that, a couple of women "looked at her funny," and she didn't want to go back. I reminded her that this was the Avoider's way of finding a way out. She jokingly said, "I hate you," and went back to the women's group.

She told me that the women in the group were "not that bad once you get to know them." In six months she had two very close friends, another rare commodity for Cynthia. She began spending more and more time with them, and they introduced her to activities she'd never done before. To her surprise she found out she was good at softball and won MVP in the last game of the season. She discovered a new passion: guitar. She'd never tried it before but realized it wasn't that tough with some practice.

I watched as the avoidant Cynthia began to disappear and a new, confident Cynthia took her place. Her grown children were pretty amazed too. They would say, "Where'd that other woman go?" She would smile back. Cynthia didn't conquer all her fears, but she refuses now to be held back. One day she asked me if I knew what a hero and a coward had in common. I asked her to tell me. "Fear," she said. The obvious point was that one chose to stay paralyzed and the other chose to move forward.

The old Cynthia still makes an appearance from time to time. But the new Cynthia takes all of Paul's statements about putting off the old man and putting on the new and applies them to her relational mask. She's realizing that sin goes much deeper than the individual choices or behaviors that one engages in. It is also found in avoidant personality traits. Difficult as this is, she is learning to "put off" this as well (see Ephesians 4:22-24).

I have worked with many Avoiders over the years. Some of them crawled out of their avoidance and made great changes. Others would try and fail and then give up (or not try at all). There are some Avoiders who will not budge regardless of how hard you push. Even Jesus had to let one go when he chose to avoid what the Lord told him to do (see Mark 10:21-22).

THE AVOIDER REDEEMED

For all their cowardice, Avoiders have something very valuable: patience. They have learned over the years to steer clear of trouble. Unfortunately they steer clear of maturity as well. What if they turned that evasive reflex against evil? The Scriptures have much to say about this:

> Dear friends, I urge you, as aliens and strangers in the world, to *abstain* from sinful desires, which war against your soul. (1 Peter 2:11, emphasis added here and following)

"But they will never follow a stranger; in fact, they will *run away* from him because they do not recognize a stranger's voice." (John 10:5)

Flee from sexual immorality. (1 Corinthians 6:18)

Therefore, my dear friends, *flee* from idolatry. (1 Corinthians 10:14)

People who want to get rich fall into temptation and a trap and into many foolish and harmful desires that plunge men into ruin and destruction. For the love of money is a root of all kinds of evil. Some people, eager for money, have wandered from the faith and pierced themselves with many griefs. But you, man of God, *flee* from all this. (1 Timothy 6:9-11)

Avoiders are practiced in the art of fleeing; it's what they do best. They are just avoiding the wrong things: responsibility, love and sacrifice. But they can learn to turn those sharpened avoiding skills against the sinful desires of people-pleasing or sexual indulgence. They can fight their proclivity toward materialism. They can turn away from the many idolatrous forces that whisper seductively to their soul. And they can run from anything that calls them away from Christ.

For Avoiders to say "I just can't do it" is a lie. It's already too late for them to claim they don't have the skill. They just need to re-train it with help from the Spirit, the Scriptures and accountable relationships. What will be new for Avoiders is learning how to become assertive. After all, if they avoid only bad stuff they are back at legalism. Life isn't found in what we avoid but in what we embrace. Grasping for healthy things requires a spiritual muscle that is underdeveloped in Avoiders, but like the rest of us, they can learn.

TIPS FOR AVOIDERS

- Realize that the job, marriage or situation you hate so much may be exactly where God wants to do his work in you.

- There is a reason you keep coming up against the same kinds of people and circumstances: God wants to work in your life *right there.*

- Understand that the Avoider never avoids pain; he only postpones it.

- Remember, courage isn't the absence of fear but the ability to walk forward anyway.

- In order for the Avoider to change, faith and obedience are crucial.

- The fact that you don't argue, struggle, embarrass yourself or take risks is not a good thing.

- Your regrets today can be traced back to issues you avoided in the past.

- Your regrets tomorrow will be traced back to issues you avoid today.

- Take heart! Jesus came to help the weak and fearful. Many heroes of the faith are former Avoiders.

How beautiful it is to see a man who is patient, easygoing *and* able to face the hard stuff. How refreshing it is to see a woman who is humble, gentle *and* capable of candor. The more you think about it, the more it sounds like the fruit of the Spirit. I appeal to my fellow Avoiders: don't let God's wonderful world pass you by out of fear that you may bleed, blush or fail. Join me as we grab life with both hands.

4

THE DEFLECTOR

Cardiophobic

Samuel is a great guy. He's funny, quick-witted and intelligent. He has no enemies; everybody likes him. Then why did Samuel come to me? Because a friend recommended he call me when he started feeling depressed. Samuel owns his own business and seems to know everybody in the construction trade. But when his depression made it hard for him to get out of bed and function at work, he knew something was wrong.

Even in his depressed state, however, Samuel had a perpetual smile on his face. Whenever he'd come to his appointments, he'd be cracking jokes and making everyone in the office laugh. As we talked about his depression, it became obvious that two things were going on: he needed medication, and he was terribly lonely. Because I'm not a doctor, I encouraged him to see one about the medication. But I am an "expert" on loneliness, so I asked him why he was lonely.

"I need a woman in my life, Russell."

"But you've been married and divorced and had lots of relationships since then."

"I know, but they never seem to last. One of us does something to mess it up, and I'm back where I started."

I knew this wasn't about being unlucky at love, so I asked him about his growing-up years. Samuel's parents had divorced when he was five, and his mother died when he was nine. It took me weeks to get this out of him because he kept skipping around to different issues. He was terrified of looking at his own heart. Samuel was a Deflector.

When I began to probe about his mother, Samuel said he felt a tremendous fear at the thought of "going there." Aha! We had found the thing he was deflecting attention from. I recommended we explore this. In the weeks that followed, a lifetime of pain and fear came pouring out of this man. This wasn't the happy-go-lucky guy everyone knew at the hardware store. This was an abandoned little boy in a grown-up body.

God began healing Samuel, but soon it became evident that there was another obstacle to Samuel's enjoying intimate relationships: his relational mask. Samuel was getting in touch with his feelings and the losses of his past, but he was still cracking the jokes and turning on the charm wherever he went. There was nothing wrong with this, per se, but for him it was a way of lying about his true feelings.

It's not that Samuel wasn't funny or witty. He was both. In fact it was his ready humor that made him so likeable; it was a God-given part of his temperament. But Samuel also used it to avoid dealing with the more painful issues of life. When his ten-year-old daughter was going through a difficult experience, he would make light of it and get her to laugh. I told him this might

> **YOU MIGHT BE A DEFLECTOR IF**
>
> - life seems like one big joke to you
> - you get nervous any time the conversation becomes serious
> - you talk a lot but say very little
> - each time someone points out a flaw, you are able to point back to them
> - your life is too busy and hectic to waste time looking at "issues"
> - your focus on everyone else (fixing, caretaking and so on) keeps the heat off you

work for a while, but eventually she would need a dad who could empathize. I pointed out to him that he was already training her to be a Deflector as well. When we began talking about the whole issue of Samuel's relational mask, I got a typical response: "Well, Russell, this is how I've always been."

"I'm not disputing that," I said, "but what if this is also a way of avoiding your pain?"

"Can you blame me?"

"Not at all, but Scripture is very clear about our need to mourn. Have you done that?"

"You mean about my mom?"

"I mean about that and a hundred other wounds you've described to me. Samuel, take a look at this verse and tell me what it means." I handed him my Bible and told him to read Ecclesiastes 7:3-4. "Sorrow is better than laughter," he read, "because a sad face is good for the heart." At this point he got a "huh?" expression on his face. I told him to continue. "The heart of the wise is in the house of mourning, but the heart of fools is in the house of pleasure."

"What does that mean?" I asked.

"I have no clue."

"Maybe it means that laughter can be a cover, and the person who uses it for that purpose isn't wise."

"Yeah, that makes sense."

I took my Bible back and turned to Proverbs 14:13. I handed it to him and asked him to read it also. "Even in laughter the heart may ache, and joy may end in grief."

"This is unreal," he said. "A week ago my accountability partner gave me the verse in James that says, 'Grieve, mourn and wail. Change your laughter to mourning and your joy to gloom.' I had no idea why he wanted me to read that, but I think it's becoming clear."

"Apparently the Holy Spirit is telling you something," I offered.

And he was. Samuel began asking God to make him honest about his joy *and* his pain. He didn't lose his sense of humor, but he began confronting the hard stuff too.

Deflectors secretly know there is pain in their past or present, but they refuse to be honest about it. As children, Deflectors make vows that sound something like this: "I will never allow this kind of pain into my heart again. I will laugh, entertain and make everyone happy. That way they will like me and life can be cheerful."

> **Deflectors secretly know there is pain in their past or present, but they refuse to be honest about it.**

This subconscious (and sometimes conscious) vow becomes the way Deflectors approach all of life. Yet the underlying pain always comes to the surface. When it does, they use sex, substances or workaholism to take the edge off. This enables them to go back to their "easygoing" demeanor. Deflectors use comedy and a "life of the party" disposition to navigate through life. Again, they have a side to their personality that is genuinely funny and positive, and God doesn't want them to change that. But he does want them to stop lying about the parts of their soul that *aren't* happy.

This is where rebellion comes in for Deflectors. They fear that if they get in touch with the pain in their soul, nobody will like them. They have taught everyone around them to expect hilarity and superficiality. Therefore, if they repent and begin living out of their truer self, the people around them will have to adjust. Some will leave. This is what Deflectors fear, not realizing that those who leave will not be people of substance anyway.

Deflectors may act happy around others, but they aren't intimate with anyone. The Deflector's husband or wife is a lonely person. The Deflector's children say they have the "coolest parent in the world," but that admiration will turn to resentment when the children need something more than a belly laugh.

Deflectors may act happy around others, but they aren't intimate with anyone.

The Deflector and the Avoider have much in common. They both avoid their true feelings. They both avoid conflict. And they both skirt around reality. There are differences, however. The Deflector has personality to spare; the Avoider is more reserved. The Deflector is a go-getter; the Avoider is isolated. If the relational masks of each were translated into hand-to-hand combat, the Avoider would absorb all your blows or run. The Deflector would deftly block each blow like a kung fu master. Each blow would be redirected away or turned back on you.

MAN, DO YOU HAVE PROBLEMS!

Deflectors take many shapes and sizes. It's easy to spot the good-time Charlie or the gal at church who is always doing great/fine/wonderful. The subtler Deflector is the wife on a campaign to straighten out her husband. What makes this kind of Deflector hard to spot is the fact that her husband's flaws are usually gargantuan. He is always a sex addict, alcoholic, verbal abuser or Avoider. His sins are very real and have the power to destroy the marriage all by themselves.

This woman's complaints are not imaginary, but therein lies the deception. In focusing on her husband's very real sins, her own can easily go unnoticed. She may say, "I know I have faults too," but she never says what those are, or she defines them nicely to make them small in comparison to his.

The fact is, her sins are just as serious (see Proverbs 20:9; Romans 2:1; 3:22-23; 1 Corinthians 10:12; James 3:2; 1 John 1:8). She takes pride in being better than he is and also fights with raging unforgiveness in her heart. Her refusal to acknowledge her controlling behavior brings great grief to God's heart, but she can't get to any of that stuff because her husband is "such a jerk." What she doesn't know is that her husband could stop all his offending behavior and things still wouldn't be okay. Those in the recovery movement call this codependency. I'm calling it deflection.

> **THINGS DEFLECTORS SAY:**
>
> "Come on, life isn't that serious!"
>
> "Sure I have my issues, but what about him?"
>
> "I'm doing great" (all the time).
>
> "I'm not selfish like they are; I take care of other people."
>
> "How about them Forty-Niners?"
>
> "I can't talk right now; I have too much to do."

Whether I cover my sins with a fetching personality or by focusing on my neighbors, it's still a diversion. In either case I cannot be intimate with others, because I am cut off from whole sections of my own heart. This is why Jesus calls us to "walk in the light" so that we can "have fellowship with one another" (1 John 1:7). Or, to say it another way, honesty and transparency are crucial to intimacy. But the Deflector has made a lifestyle out of her core belief that "honesty always brings abandonment."

THE DEFLECTOR REDEEMED

We've established that the sin of Deflectors is dishonesty. They consistently tell lies about themselves by being cheerful and "up" all the time. Of course, this breaks down occasionally, and Deflectors then become Aggressors. But for the most part, they deflect attention away from their own reality—or at least away from any reality that doesn't fit their "I'm doing great" relational mask.

So what skills do Deflectors have that they can use against their own sin, to the betterment of others? Peter gives us a clue: "Above all, love each other deeply, because love covers over a multitude of sins" (1 Peter 4:8). Deflectors are skilled at covering over the sins and pain of their own heart, but what if they took that skill and covered the sins of those around them? What if, like the father of the prodigal son, they deflected attention away from the crimes of the sinner and celebrated the sinner's worth instead (see Luke 15:21-23)?

What if, instead of trying to make everybody feel happy, the Deflector made everybody feel loved—loved in the true biblical sense? Not the "you're wonderful and can do no wrong" jive that he tells everyone, but an honest love reflected through steady eyes? Yes, people need to know about their sins. But most of them can't hear us when we point them out, because their shame is already drowning out whatever we would say. What cuts a path through shame? Only one thing: piercing, robust love.

Real love isn't syrupy; it's scary.

Real love isn't syrupy; it's scary. Think of the times you've been truly loved. Chances are you felt either elated or extremely uncomfortable. Deflectors don't want anyone to feel uncomfortable, but if they won't subject others to this, they cannot truly love them. Once when Jesus looked down at Peter with eyes brimming over with love, Peter couldn't stand it and begged him to leave. But Jesus didn't flinch. He stood there cutting Peter's shame to ribbons and told him, "Don't be afraid; from now on you will catch men" (Luke 5:8-10).

Deflectors who catch this vision won't pretend that others aren't sinful. In fact, when they learn how to *really* love, they won't shy away from addressing the sins of others. Like our Lord, they will call it what it is but not use it to grind others into the dirt. They will know that their shame is already doing that.

Like Jesus with the woman at the well, they will be able to say, "The man you now have is not your husband," but they won't launch into a sermon on the evils of adultery. They will, like our Lord, tell others there is fulfillment for the thirst that drives the sin (see John 4:10-18). They will know that the sinner in front of them needs the reassurance of love. They will discern when the drug addict, town slut or self-righteous legalist needs to have his or her system shocked by grace rather than burdened even more by unbearable guilt.

This is a fine art that requires finesse. It isn't "sloppy agape." It is a clear-eyed and deliberate attack on the shame of others, utilizing the only effective weapon there is. Remember, Peter didn't say, "Above all, shame each other deeply," which is what many of us do in the name of "holiness." He told us to *love* deeply; this alone covers sin.

Deflectors will learn how to stop drawing attention away from their own reality and the reality of others. They will learn to stop using others' faults as a distraction from their own. They will also learn to take negative realities into consideration and never *lie* about them. Yet they will deflect attention away from the lesser realities while pointing to the greater.

What I am saying might be misunderstood by some as a softening on sin. Hear me well: sin is a deadly business, and we cannot take it lightly. The cross is proof of how serious it is to our God. There is surely a time to call a person's actions what they are, without mincing words. But many of us, in our righteous zeal, walk up to the "bruised reeds" in our midst and give them a final snap (Isaiah 42:3). Or we take what little spark is left in their wick and snuff it out in the name of exhortation. As I said, doing it right takes a lot of skill. But God is calling the lifelong Deflector to deflect attention away from the sins that torment the guilty and to pound them with God's grace instead.

For any of this to happen, however, Deflectors will have to embrace the negative, painful, frightening realities of their own sin or pain. But they must not stop there. They must go on to the greater reality of God's healing, forgiving love through the blood of Jesus. Recovering Deflectors will learn to dwell on the negatives only long enough to address them honestly and then move on to the greatest reality of all: God's indescribable love for them. They will make it their business to deflect attention away from all lesser realities as soon as it is appropriate. When they learn to do this in their personal life, they will be able to extend it to others.

> **THINGS DEFLECTORS DO:**
>
> - constantly crack jokes, tell stories and so on
> - switch from fun-loving to furious in a second
> - talk about everything but their feelings
> - make themselves indispensable to the church, company or group
> - immerse themselves so deeply in jobs or children as to make other relationships impossible

FROM MOURNING TO DANCING

Each year our staff and several participants from our ministry attend a conference. This event is known for its honest and powerful worship times. I was pleased that Benny was able to come along. Benny and I had done a lot of good work, but he was definitely a Deflector. One night during a general session we entered into a time of extended worship. The presence of the Holy Spirit was thick. I saw Benny a few chairs over, obviously weeping. I pushed through the other worshipers so I could talk with him.

"What's happening, Ben? Can you tell me?" I asked.

"Oh, Russell, I feel his love!" He could barely get the words out.

Benny dissolved into my arms heaving powerful sobs. I knew I was just supposed to hold him. We stood there for what seemed like an hour. When the service was over, I asked him what God had done.

"Russell," he said, "I've always known in my head that Jesus loves me, but I've never experienced *this*."

For the rest of that evening he couldn't talk about it without tearing up again. We talked late into the night about the deep wounds in his soul left by childhood abandonment. Benny had obviously been touched in those very spots.

"But I am afraid of one thing," he confessed. "I'm afraid it won't last. I'm afraid that tomorrow I will wake up and discover that it was just an emotional high." I understood Benny's fears. Everyone else in his life had left him; why should God be any different?

I reassured him that this wasn't a temporary high. I encouraged him to continue spending time with the Lord throughout the week and to journal about what God was saying to him. Several times during that week I spotted Benny sitting under a tree, writing furiously in his notebook. Some time after our return home, I met with him again. I asked if the Lord had "left him."

"I don't walk around in that glorious fog every day," Benny told me. "But something *happened* to me at the conference—and it's still there."

I've been able to observe Benny's life since then. In these three years he has lost much of his fear. He can still cut up with the best of them, but he is honest now about his emotions. He is no longer threatened by feelings of anger or disappointment. He realizes that these are just feelings that alert him to some old belief still lurking inside.

Gone is the man who had to cover his reality with a funny story. He is learning how to admit his genuine pain whenever it arises. More often than not, Benny talks about some new way Jesus is loving him. God has taken him from laughter to mourning and back to laughter again.

TIPS FOR DEFLECTORS

- As strange as it sounds, being "nice" may be a sin for you.

- Meet with a pastor or counselor to see what you are deflecting *away from*.

- If all you think or talk about is someone else, you are deflecting. Turn the spotlight around.

- Jesus is neither ashamed nor afraid of those things you hide. Let him into those areas too.

- Find someone who is straightforward to be accountable to.

- When you are with others, practice *not* being charming, funny or smart.

- Resist the urge to say or do something every time a situation becomes tense.

- Remember, Jesus hides your sins—you don't have to.

5

THE SELF-BLAMER

Worshiper of the Darkness

Mary hated the way her husband talked to the kids. His idea of discipline was to say, "What's the matter with you!" She saw their self-esteem wilting beneath his abusive tirades. Whenever she tried to talk with James about this, it always became an argument. But on this particular morning he'd been unusually cruel. She knew she had to say something.

"Honey, I know the kids can do some stupid things, but when you talk that way, I'm concerned about the damage it does."

"Here we go again!" he yelled. "I can never do anything right with these kids. It would be better for me to keep my mouth shut and let *you* be the parent."

Whenever James reacted this way (which was often), the conversation always came to a grinding halt. He would go on and on about what an unfit parent he was. Mary would try to tell him that this wasn't her point. She only wanted James to take a look at why he got so mad and do something to change it, but he never did; he just wallowed in his "worthlessness," and Mary would walk away feeling frustrated and angry. Nothing she said or did broke through this impenetrable wall. James was a Self-Blamer.

VICTIMS AND VICTIMIZERS

Every Self-Blamer I've ever counseled was an abuse victim. They came from homes where their self-esteem was attacked through verbal, physical or sexual abuse. Whether the abuse was obvious or subtle, they somehow concluded it was their fault. When children are consistently mistreated, they automatically internalize that as a statement about them. They don't have the insight to say, "Daddy treats me that way because something is broken in him." Instead they say, "Daddy does that because I am a bad kid."

> **YOU MIGHT BE A SELF-BLAMER IF**
>
> - you think constantly about your failure, stupidity or sinfulness
> - you always seem to mess things up (just like you knew you would!)
> - you see yourself as a lost cause
> - as far as you are concerned, everyone else is smarter, more godly or more disciplined than you are
> - you believe that God is mad, disappointed or disgusted with you
> - guilt is your constant companion

The psychological and spiritual damage is real. God's heart breaks for the defenseless child who has to live through this. David referred to these hurting souls when he said to God, "The victim commits himself to you" (Psalm 10:14). For too long the body of Christ has been in denial about the very real pain of such victims. Thankfully that day is ending. We now provide counseling and ministry to those who have experienced such debilitating wounds.

As real as the shame and inner pain can be to the victim, there also can be a very dark side to it. Many of these children grow up to be women and men who feel inwardly worthless *and hide behind that.* As with the relational masks we've already described, the Self-Blamer doesn't do this consciously, but there *is* a benefit to being "worthless": it protects you from having to grow. If I am despicable and stupid, then you certainly can't expect me to change my behavior! I'm too ignorant and broken even to know where to start, the Self-Blamer says.

The husband or wife of the Self-Blamer intuitively knows that the whimpers of "I'm hopeless; I'll never get it" hide a refusal to face the issues. But if they try to point this out, it only sounds like more condemnation, and another fight ensues. The children of the Self-Blaming parent are put in an awful place too. When they are young they feel grieved and responsible that Daddy or Mommy feels the way they do and attempt never to upset them. But, being children, they fail. When they do, the Self-Blaming parent reacts with verbal or physical violence. The parent then lapses into "I'm such a failure; how could I hurt you like that?" and the child has to reassure the adult through direct comfort or renewed efforts at being good.

If you meet Self-Blamers at church or Bible study, you will be struck by their seeming honesty and humility. They say, "I know I'm not right with God. I don't know how he puts up with me." This elicits a couple of responses from those around them. They respond with a sympathetic, "Oh, don't say that. It isn't true." Or they respond with an impressed awe. "Most people won't admit their failures," they say, "but Francis knows she's a sinner and isn't afraid to admit it."

MATURAPHOBIC

Self-Blamers have heard the condemning, demeaning voices for so long that they now are their own. Each time they try to move toward maturity and fail, the voice says, "See, you are so stupid. You will never do anything right. Why even try?" This isn't just a "poor me" syndrome; Self-Blamers feel this from every cell of their being. One Self-Blamer I talked to said, "Russell, this isn't my belief about myself. It's really how I am." When I pointed out to her that she knew others who said the same thing, she told me why it wasn't true for them. The strongholds that control our lives are irrational and inconsistent, but we are committed to them nonetheless.

Self-Blamers are terrified of maturity, believing they are incapable
of stepping out of their comfort zone. In reality they are just inexperienced. I was camping at a river near Shaver Lake, California, recently. We hiked to a spot where people were jumping off a
twenty-foot rock into the water. A few teenage boys did it, plus a girl
and a couple of men. There was one girl, however, who kept coming
to the edge and looking over only to say, "I can't do it."

**The strongholds that control our lives
are irrational and inconsistent,
but we are committed to them nonetheless.**

Those of us on the shore encouraged her and told her she could.
When the peer pressure became too much, she'd step to the edge and
start breathing heavily, only to back down again. Her dad yelled up
to her, "You can do it, Sally! Think of the bragging rights you'll have!"
I could tell she really wanted to, but the fear was suffocating her.
Someone else shouted, "Don't think. Just jump!"

She needed one more push, so I started the chant: "Sal-ly! Sal-ly!"
Twenty more joined in, and a new determination formed on her face.
She stepped forward, then back again, then forward and—out into
space she went. She shot into the river like a bullet and next thing we
knew she was breaking the surface shouting, "Woo hoo! I *did* it!" The
group of friends and strangers broke into applause as a
twelve-year-old found her pluck.

We've all been where Sally was. We've stared a risk in the face and
said, "I can't do it," but that wasn't true. We may have been scared out
of our minds. We may have been sure we would die. Our bodies and
minds may have been paralyzed with fear, but we did have the *ability*.
What we didn't have was the experience. Unfortunately there's only

one way to get that. Sally pushed past every "reality" that held her feet to that rock and jumped into the arms of adventure.

Self-Blamers crawl down off the rock in self-imposed shame and disgrace. "I just couldn't do it," they say. "I know everybody else can, but I can't. I'm such a coward." Since we all know what it feels like to be terrified, we can empathize, but in reality Self-Blamers choose their own inward reality over the possibility of success. This is where the rebellion comes in. Their terror is genuine, but their inability to take a risk *isn't*. Like the Avoider and the Deflector, the Self-Blamer allows fear to be lord, rather than Christ: "'Do not fear what they fear; do not be frightened.' But in your hearts set apart Christ as Lord" (1 Peter 3:14-15).

CHOOSE YOU THIS DAY

The most abused man I've ever counseled was a Self-Blamer. Nathan was the son of a very conservative pastor. In Nathan's church you couldn't listen to rock music, grow your hair below the collar or even lean in the direction of "the world." Not only were he and his brother expected to be good examples, they were also, in their father's mind, a direct reflection on his spirituality. Anything that reflected poorly on their father was greeted with outright abuse.

Once when Nathan was at a friend's house, a Beatles song was played on the radio. Instead of running out of the house as he knew he was supposed to, he sat there feeling a mixture of pleasure and fear. When he got home he "confessed" the whole thing and was punched in the face repeatedly by his father. His brother stepped in but not before Nathan's jaw was broken. Not only did dad physically abuse his sons, he also abused them sexually.

Not surprisingly, both sons grew up to have major problems. They turned to drugs, sex and "worldliness," and both were in and out of Christian rehab ministries. Nathan's brother became an Aggressor.

His violent, out-of-control behavior landed him in jail several times. Nathan's temperament was different, however. He didn't take his anger out on those around him; he turned it inward. Both men had been taught to hate themselves. They differed only in how they expressed it.

Nathan tried to "do it right." He found a church with a very strong, authoritarian pastor (coincidence?) and got involved in ministry. He married a divorced woman with two kids, and they had one of their own. Things seemed to be fine for a while. Shelly and Nathan had Bible studies in their home, and Nathan led worship on his guitar. It wasn't long, however, before Nathan began drifting back into drugs and prostitution. Shelly was heartbroken but willing to work it out.

> **THINGS SELF-BLAMERS SAY:**
>
> "I have no idea why you love me."
>
> "I can't do anything right."
>
> "God must think I'm an idiot."
>
> "I should've known it wouldn't succeed."
>
> "I knew it was too good to be true."
>
> "What's it all about, anyway?"

Nathan told her, "I'm no good. Why do you even stay with me?" Shelly said she loved him no matter what. But after three more years of drugs and infidelity, even Shelly's love couldn't endure. When they divorced, Nathan went back to his old addictions with a vengeance. His downward slide came to a halt the night he propositioned a hooker who turned out to be a cop. Nathan's name was in the paper, and his face was on the news. What he'd always believed about himself was now public knowledge: he was a hopeless reprobate.

It was after his arrest that he came to me for the first time. Nathan was absolutely starving for the grace of God. I gave him as much as he could bear. When he would confess some unpardonable sin, I would counter with the blood of Jesus. He knew all about that, he would tell me, but *his* sins were different. Getting him to move forward was like convincing a donkey to pull her rear off the ground.

Then suddenly a light came on. After hearing for months about a God who loved and forgave sinners, he had an experience at work. One of the tenants at the mobile home park where he was a grounds-keeper had lost her dog. It was the most precious thing in the world to this elderly woman. Everyone who could walk was out searching for it. Nathan felt an uncharacteristic boldness to ask God to let him find the dog. He walked two blocks away from the park and, to his surprise, spotted the animal in a yard. When he called it by name, it ran into his arms.

When Nathan walked back into the park, a very grateful woman met him. Through tears she said, "Thank you, thank you," over and over as she clutched her only friend. Nathan felt something very strange growing inside him: joy. He had prayed and God had showed him where the dog was. What were the odds? As simple as this was, Nathan took it as proof that maybe he wasn't worthless after all.

When he shared this with the counseling group, all eyes lit up. Finally it wasn't us telling him that he was loved by God, but he was telling us. Nathan seemed to have a new confidence after that. Not a week went by when he didn't share something that God was revealing about his belovedness. "I'm feeling like the most special person in the world!" he said. We couldn't have been happier.

Not surprisingly, Nathan's bad habits began to fade as well. He was instructing all of us about how God's grace "teaches us to say 'No' to ungodliness and worldly passions, and to live self-controlled, upright and godly lives" (Titus 2:11-12). We laughed as the student became the teacher. Things went well until he fell into one of his old sins. When that happened, I reminded him of the grace he'd been experiencing, but he was inconsolable. "I *knew* this would happen!" he said. "I *knew* it couldn't last."

I knew exactly where he was heading. He began "slipping up"

more often and lamenting how contemptible he was. When he began missing appointments, I knew his old relational mask was back. As much as he seemed to hate this way of living, it brought a strange comfort to him as well. It really was easier for Nathan to embrace his dad's vision of him rather than his Father's vision.

The old conditioning and programming is real for Self-Blamers, but they are not without participation in the process. Our Lord understands how difficult this battle is for us. He's under no delusion that simply reciting Bible verses will make everything all right. He expects a hundred hands to try to peel our fingers off his truth, but he tells us emphatically, "If you *hold* to my teaching, you are really my disciples" (John 8:31, emphasis added). He doesn't say, "When forces external and internal assault you, go ahead and let go. It's too hard to hold on anyway."

**We must let God change the
very fabric of our hearts.
To the degree that we drag our feet in this process,
we miss the abundant life here on earth.**

In another place he tells us bluntly: "Hold on to instruction, do not let it go; guard it well, for it is your life" (Proverbs 4:13). Jesus isn't telling Self-Blamers (or anyone else) that they have to overcome this or they are bound for hell. He is saying that getting rid of the "big" sins is not enough; we must let God change the very fabric of our hearts. To the degree that we drag our feet in this process, we miss the abundant life here on earth.

HATE YOUR NEIGHBOR

Not only that, but to the degree that I allow my sinful relational mask to continue, I choose not to love those around me. If I am an Avoider, I avoid three things: God, the reality of my heart and the love-needs of those around me. If I am a Deflector, I refuse to engage my pain and the true pain of others. If I am a Self-Blamer, I criticize myself endlessly but don't do what is necessary to change. If I continue to wear these relational masks, I will never develop the character required to genuinely love those around me.

Isn't it remarkable that we can stop drinking, smoking and being "bad" people but still allow these deficient coping styles to continue? These ways of interacting undermine the very foundation of our faith:

> "Love the Lord your God with all your heart and with all your soul and with all your mind and with all your strength." The second [command] is this: "Love your neighbor as yourself." There is no commandment greater than these. (Mark 12:30-31)

There is no commandment greater than these? That's what our Lord said. So if we tithe, pray six hours a day, evangelize everything that moves and avoid every bad movie at the multiplex but miss this key point, we miss the whole point. Yet this is what thousands of us who pride ourselves on being Christians do every day.

It's easy to miss this because it isn't as obvious as more socially unacceptable sins within the church. We also miss it because it is so ingrained in us. Our unique relational masks don't seem like masks at all; they are as natural to us as a heartbeat. But the fact that something seems normal and un-

THINGS SELF-BLAMERS DO:

- give up
- live in self-pity
- attract Saviors
- exasperate those who try to help
- turn over a new leaf (short-lived)
- see God as a critical, perfectionist parent

chosen doesn't mean that Jesus doesn't want to master it. Maybe this is where the rubber meets the road when it comes to lordship. No wonder so many opt for legalism instead.

NOW FOR SOME GOOD NEWS

I have to be blunt about this for two reasons. Number one, because most Christians aren't. And number two, because our Lord is. Once, when two of his disciples copped an attitude, he rebuked them and said, "You do not know what kind of spirit you are of" (Luke 9:55). Was he referring to their spirit or to demonic spirits? Probably both. That's rather unsettling when you think about it. That Satan can use our unrecognized relational masks should make all of us think.

Where's the good news in all this? It is found in the relational masks themselves. As unworkable and unloving as they are, they also hold—under God—the secret to our liberation. It's not that Avoiders must stop their avoidance. They must turn their polished avoiding skills against the right things. Deflectors aren't called by God to abandon all deflection but to understand reality and deflect falsehood. Self-Blamers aren't required to stop all blaming but to blame the right things in the right ways.

When Nathan went into his downward spiral, he dropped out of sight for about two years. The other day I found this encouraging message on my answering machine: "Russell, it's me, Nathan. I know I haven't seen you for a long time, but I'm ready to come back and really deal with my issues. I hope you still want to see me."

When he came, I greeted him warmly and told him I was so happy to see him. He was sheepish at first, but I could tell something was different. He looked, well, more adult. He told me that he'd fallen into all the same old stuff. It got old pretty fast, he said. Now he wanted to deal with things not because of his wife or the courts but because he was starting to think maybe he was worth it. Nathan still goes up and down, but he's doing one hundred percent better than before.

THE SELF-BLAMER REDEEMED

What are Self-Blamers good at? They are good at hating. They are experts at loathing themselves and their every weakness. They have a bitter and passionate disgust for their own humanity and failings. The Self-Blamer is practiced and skilled at self-hate. Most Christians would have a hard time seeing any place in the Christian life for hatred. But they would be mistaken. Hate is crucial for spiritual growth and victory:

There is a time for everything,
and a season for every activity under heaven:
. . . a time to love and a time to hate. (Ecclesiastes 3:1, 8)

Let those who love the LORD hate evil. (Psalm 97:10)

To fear the LORD is to hate evil;
I hate pride and arrogance,
evil behavior and perverse speech. (Proverbs 8:13)

Love must be sincere. Hate what is evil; cling to what is good.
(Romans 12:9)

There are six things the LORD hates,
seven that are detestable to him:
haughty eyes,
a lying tongue,
hands that shed innocent blood,
a heart that devises wicked schemes,
feet that are quick to rush into evil,
a false witness who pours out lies
and a man who stirs up dissension among brothers.
(Proverbs 6:16-19)

The man who loves his life will lose it, while the man who hates his life in this world will keep it for eternal life. (John 12:25)

Christians cannot live a life that pleases God unless they develop a passionate sense of hate. Self-Blamers are already ahead of the game. Hatred is the driving force of their heart. Hating is the one thing they do well. Here's the problem: they hate the wrong thing. Due to abuse and faulty thinking, Self-Blamers have come to have contempt for their own soul. They hate everything about themselves: body, soul and spirit.

Christians cannot live a life that pleases God unless they develop a passionate sense of hate.

What if Self-Blamers realized that they have been lied to and got mad about *that?* What if they declared war on all feelings of hate directed toward anything God finds precious? What if they decided to love what God loves and hate what God hates? Self-Blamers are uniquely skilled at doing this, if they so choose.

It won't be easy to throw off years of conditioning, but it can be done. Self-Blamers believe that they really *are* worthless. They believe that the realities of their lives have taught them this. In actuality, their self-hate is a childish interpretation of the pain of their past. In other words, their self-contempt is a conclusion that they've drawn and embraced until it has become their identity.

There is good news in this. A view that Self-Blamers adopt is a view they can discard. It will take much work and submission to Jesus' teaching (something they are not good at, which they hate themselves for!), but, like every new attitude and behavior, it can be learned.

The answer for Self-Blamers is not to eradicate hate from their life but to unplug it from themselves and direct it at those things God commands them to hate. We've already established that hatred is biblical. What is not biblical is the type of hatred that most of us practice. We hate people that hurt our feelings. We hate the Democrats or the Republicans. We hate homosexuals or Muslims. In other words, our hatred is often directed at individuals or groups.

Biblical hatred is directed at evil. We continue struggling in our hearts with "flesh and blood" when the Scriptures tell us that the battle is not located there (Ephesians 6:12). We are to hate the demonic. We are to hate the evil in us and the evil in others. We are to hate injustice, lying, egotism and everything else that strengthens this fantasy we call "the real world." Self-Blamers, prior to repentance, hate what God loves (themselves and others). After repentance they hate what God hates and no longer throw the baby out with the bathwater.

Self-Blamers who are undoing their relational mask will stop berating themselves and hate only their sins. They will begin loving those around them but hating the satanic and carnal forces that influence them. They will declare a quiet war on all things that are detestable to God. They will especially hate those teachings, influences and attitudes that grind others into the dirt. Whether these influences come from the culture, the media, the family or the church, they will quietly work to tear them apart.

The Self-Blamer can become an iconoclast. Centuries ago an iconoclast was a person dedicated to the destruction of idols. Of course, this was taken too far, and the iconoclasts of the past destroyed beautiful works of art in the name of the Lord. "Idols every one!" they claimed. The iconoclasts of the past made the same mistake modern iconoclasts make: destroying the symbol but leaving the underlying power untouched.

Self-Blamers who grasp what is being said here can become a true iconoclast in the tradition of the apostles and reformers. They can nurse a hatred for all things anti-Christ and antihuman and work to destroy them. This is what it means to hate evil and cling to good.

But Self-Blamers in recovery must always be on guard against the temptation to begin hating people again (including themselves). They must know who the enemy really is and not be tempted to go after the wrong things.

Marla is one Self-Blamer who is coming to understand this. Her husband divorced her because she had an affair. He had one too, but somehow his wasn't as serious in his mind. He moved in with another woman and left Marla on her own to care for three kids. Marla blamed herself for everything. I pointed out to her that she certainly played her part but she couldn't take all the credit.

A kind man from her church began helping her with bills and doing things with the kids. She was so grateful. When he pressured her for sex, she felt she "owed" it to him and gave in. She told me how stupid she was and how much she hated herself for being weak. Marla saw all the evil in herself but never saw it in others.

She had indeed made foolish choices, but they were all based on her belief that she had to make everyone happy, no matter the cost. I helped her see that taking care of herself was not selfish but mandatory. She has taken to that truth like a woman possessed. "No more people-pleasing!" she told me. "From now on I'm taking care of *me*."

As narcissistic as this may sound, it's actually an improvement for her. Now she asks the Lord to show her who he is. In the process she's learning who *she* is too. She is preferring her children over any man. And she is setting healthy boundaries for the very first time in her life. The helpless victim that she once was is being replaced by a woman who isn't easily fooled. She is learning that she can't take care of others if she can't take care of herself.

Recovering Self-Blamers will learn that the passion that once fueled their hate can now fuel their love. In fact, there is no real love without hate. If I love you, I will hate anything that tries to destroy you. As Self-Blamers understand this more and more, they will develop a balance of passionate love for God, people and all things good. A corresponding hatred for all things that draw us away from loving God and others will grow as well. Once again, this is the balanced, Spirit-filled life that Scripture encourages us to live. As Self-Blamers wrap their heart around these truths, they will no longer focus on their negative self (I'm so evil, dirty, stupid, fat and so on); they will focus on Jesus Christ and destroy the idol of self-hatred.

TIPS FOR SELF-BLAMERS

- If this chapter describes you, don't shame yourself for it!
- Your sin and failure is not the most powerful force in the universe. God's love is.
- Find a counselor who can help you discover where you picked up these negative messages.
- If you fight with anxiety or depression, talk with your doctor. (Yes, even Christians need medication sometimes.)
- Fight the hateful self-talk and fine-tune your heart to the affirming voice of God.
- Stop dismissing those who affirm you as well-intentioned fools.
- Remember, Jesus came for the losers, the dropouts and the hopeless (see Mark 2:17; Luke 4:17-21; 1 Corinthians 1:27-29).

6

THE SAVIOR

Idolatry of Serving

Maria was grieved to hear about Judith. Though Judith wasn't her favorite person in the world, she did feel compassion when informed of Judith's total hysterectomy and the complications that followed. When they had gone to church together, Judith had said and done some things that were very painful for Maria. That's why Maria changed churches, but now a year had gone by, and she was aware that her former friend was in pain. She had to call.

"Hello, Judith? It's Maria. I heard about the surgery. How are you doing?"

"Oh, thank you for calling, Maria. I haven't heard from you forever. Well, the surgery went okay, but I've had a lot of bleeding. The doctor has ordered bed rest, and I'm being a good girl."

"Well, if there's anything I can do, let me know."

"Actually, Maria, I'm glad you called. The biggest problem in my life right now is not my health; it's my marriage."

"Oh?" Maria answered.

"Yes, I've been struggling all day, and I didn't know who to talk to—then *you* called."

"What's happening, Judith? How can I help?"

"Well . . . I don't know how to say this. I caught Will using pornography last night. Turns out he's been doing it for a long time, and

I . . . I . . ." Judith's words squeezed into sobs.

Maria was stunned, not because of what Judith said but because she had been through exactly the same thing. She knew the shock, betrayal and slow, painful healing that Judith was about to experience. She knew exactly what to say, but she didn't say it. She was frozen. *If I tell Judith what she needs to hear, I'm going to have to expose myself,* Maria thought. *It's obvious that she's in pain, but I'm not sure I want to take a chance that she'll hurt me again.*

Maria commiserated with her former friend and promised to pray for her. She gave her the name of a counselor and said goodbye. When she hung up, she felt like a flaming hypocrite. *Why do I feel so awful when all I wanted to do was help?* She felt very disturbed and knew that something wasn't right, but what was it? "Lord, I felt sure you wanted me to call Judith, but now I'm just confused. What happened?"

The Spirit's answer was immediate and direct: "You lied." Maria knew that was it. She hadn't called Judith because she really cared. She called because that's what she was "supposed" to do. Maria had always helped people. It's what she did. But when push came to shove she wouldn't give this woman what she really needed most: honesty. Maria loved helping others unless it involved becoming vulnerable. For the first time in her life she realized that her "ministry" was less about others and more about her. Now she was the one crying.

LET ME HELP YOU

If you met Maria, several things would

YOU MIGHT BE A SAVIOR IF

- you believe everyone else's need is more important than your own
- you are a workaholic
- you love serving God and others but occasionally resent it
- you have a hard time delegating tasks
- you see "fun" as a waste of time
- you are hurt when others fail to acknowledge your sacrifices

strike you. First, you would see a statuesque woman with short, black hair framing a very pleasant face. Second, you would see a woman who is very sweet and considerate. Third, once you got to know her, you would see that she has an incredible heart for God. So what's the problem? The problem with Maria and the thousands of brothers and sisters in her fraternity is this: they live in fear and dishonesty.

Saviors are all around us. We've been blessed and offended by them—sometimes within the same five minutes. Saviors believe it is their job to help anyone who may be in need. This sounds very noble, but here's where the deception comes in: they do this to avoid dealing with their own pain.

Saviors have no idea this is happening, just as the Avoiders, Deflectors and Self-Blamers have no idea that their relational masks are a flight from maturity. Saviors have been programmed to be there for others and to find their identity in this. When they can't help someone, it makes them very uneasy. If you try to help the Savior, look out! They will either say with a smile, "Thank you, but I'm fine," or they will get very defensive that you even insinuated they needed help at all.

I said Saviors live in fear. What are they afraid of? They are afraid of having needs. In fact, if you ask them what they need, they usually can't answer. They are not in touch with their own needs (a detachment they mistake for humility or spirituality). So they fixate on the needs of others in an attempt to find their place in the world through service. A great example of this is the famous story of Mary and Martha (Luke 10:38-42).

Martha became downright indignant when Jesus didn't command her sister, Mary, to get up and help in the kitchen. Why did she get so bent out of shape? Because Martha found her worth and value as a person in "doing" for others. The fact that Jesus didn't jump on board caused Martha to question the value of her service and, hence, her *own* value. How puzzled (and secretly offended) Martha must have been when Jesus said that Mary made the better choice.

Saviors are afraid of having needs.

To Saviors it seems weak to "worry about your own needs." They see their needs as unimportant, but strangely, the needs of others are huge. How do you explain this inconsistency? If the people around me have valid needs that I should meet, doesn't it stand to reason that my needs are just as valid? It should, but not to the Savior. The Savior has come to believe that neediness is equal to weakness. So what appears to be a sacrificial act on the part of the Savior is really an insult. *I will help you because you are so pathetic and weak, but I don't need anyone to help me.*

This is also where the dishonesty and pride come in. Anyone who believes he or she doesn't need the help of others is living in a fantasy. Secretly, Saviors know they have needs, but they are ashamed of them. They've been taught in their families that what they want or value is irrelevant.

Robert was raised in such a home. He was the oldest of five siblings. His dad was an alcoholic and a workaholic, so Robert became the surrogate father of the family. His mother just felt overwhelmed most of the time. Robert was very sensitive to his mother's unhappiness and filled in the gaps around the house. When his mother was depressed or tired, he jumped in to take care of the other kids or do the cleaning. His mother would always say, "You're my helper. You're such a *good* boy."

Robert's parents didn't have the wisdom or the desire to learn how to meet *his* needs. This left him to scratch around on his own, getting validation any way he could. When Robert got older, he even volunteered at a children's hospital. He would take the little ones on his lap and read to them. He gave out what he never had in hopes that it would come back to him, but, as with most Saviors, people just took advantage of him until he had nothing left to give.

Not surprisingly, Robert cycled through two marriages before he figured out that he was never going to save the women in his life. Instead of being grateful for his "kind and noble service," his wives always came to resent him instead, as did his children. He couldn't make any sense of it. Why did people treat him this way when all he ever did was give?

Saviors believe they are loving others, but they are mistaken. What they are really doing is being kind, nice and sweet so that others will appreciate them. It's been called codependency, enabling and a host of other things. But it is not love. Love is working for the spiritual growth of the person next to you. Let me give you the classic analogy of a Savior at work, who is "loving" her spouse.

Imagine someone with a drinking problem. He stays out late, misses work, collapses in his own vomit and piles up traffic tickets. The Savior wife will have dinner ready for him, call his boss, clean him up and make sure his traffic fines get paid. She believes this is loving. Actually, she is enabling him to get deeper into a self-destructive cycle. *Real* love requires that she do what she can to stop this cycle, not perpetuate it. But the Savior feels powerless to do this because it would involve huge changes to her lifestyle and personality. She denies this and goes on in the belief that her "love" will win him over in time.

I've described one type of Savior—the sweet, enabling kind. There are others. Some Saviors aren't as subtle as Maria or Robert. They are more obvious in the way they control the people around them. They can be pushy, self-righteous or downright manipulative. We often

call people like this "control freaks,"
but the sweet Savior and the
not-so-subtle Savior have this in common: they both want to help others.
The love of God is in there somewhere, but it's intertwined with a lot of
manipulation, fear and unbelief.

FEAR-BASED MINISTRY

Saviors often have great faith in some
areas, but in other areas their core belief is "God can't be trusted." Because
they don't trust God to work in the
lives of others, they sign themselves
up as his helpers. Much of what we
call ministry today is institutionalized Saviorhood.

> **THINGS SAVIORS SAY:**
>
> "Sure, I'll do it."
>
> "Well, *somebody* has to be responsible around here!"
>
> "I have my faults too" (but no "big" sins are ever listed).
>
> "I just have a lot of compassion."
>
> "I'm glad *other* people get to take vacations!"
>
> "When is it going to be *my* turn?" (said only under extreme pressure).

This will make more sense if you remember the definition of love:
working for the spiritual growth of another. If you want another person to grow in Christ, is it wise to nag him, shame him or harp on
him about how he needs to pray and read the Bible? Is this really a
good motivation for the spiritual disciplines? Apparently in most
churches it is. People are told from pulpits and Sunday school classes
the world over that they need to tithe, evangelize and "get serious
about God."

This indeed gets a lot of people moving, but does it produce
genuine, heartfelt intimacy with Jesus Christ? No. It produces a
smooth-running evangelistic machine that ministry leaders can be
proud of. But what if the people in our church or ministry really need
to know that they are loved even if they aren't doing "the stuff"? Are
we willing to care for them, pray for them and *wait* for them? What
they really need is to grow from the inside out. But the pastor or min-

istry leader who does this may look like a passive "liberal."

Now you can see why real love is harder to give than the counterfeit offering of the Savior. Jesus, the *real* Savior, was constantly criticized by those who felt he was too soft on sin and too kind to people who needed to get with the program. For instance, he didn't rebuke the woman at the well (in spite of her obvious immorality). Instead he told her that he could meet her need if she wanted him to (John 4:1-30). Later he passed up the chance to tell another woman to stop her reckless lifestyle. Rather he let her express her affection in a way that respectable society deemed inappropriate (Luke 7:36-50). And he showered his love on her in return.

Jesus didn't seem too concerned about whether people did it "correctly." He was concerned about whether people knew they were loved. In divine wisdom he understood that if people were loved—and really knew it—they would change. They would root out the selfishness in their lives and even die if they knew they were safe in his love. He wasn't (and isn't) above rebuking one whom he loves, but he never does it because we embarrass him or fail to meet his expectations. He does it because strong medicine may be what we need in that particular occasion.

> **Jesus didn't seem too concerned about whether people did it "correctly." He was concerned about whether people knew they were loved.**

Remember when he rebuked Peter and called him "Satan" (Matthew 16:21-23)? Did he do that because Peter ticked him off? Did he do that because Peter dared discourage him from embracing the cross? Did he do that because Peter should have known better and it frustrated him? No. Our Lord did that because he was committed to

Peter's spiritual growth at that moment and for the rest of Peter's life. Peter needed to know that the syrupy sentimentality at work in his heart was not love but a desire to maintain the status quo.

It was understandable for Peter to feel this way; he didn't know that the cross was crucial to everything Jesus was about. Peter also needed to know that in the future he would be tempted to choose comfort over pain. Jesus intentionally spoke these stinging words so that they would never leave Peter's memory. The Lord knew that one day Peter would have a cross of his own, and he was already preparing Peter for it. This is love. It can be blunt when it needs to be, but only if that is what the other person really needs in order to move into his God-given future.

Saviors often get critical when compassion is needed or mushy when a clear word of direction is in order. They do this because they don't understand the nature of real love; they haven't allowed God to love them at their point of deepest need. They feel weak and pathetic for even having that need, remember? So why would they bring it to Jesus and expect him to touch it? That would be "selfish." And if Saviors know anything, they know that being selfish is bad.

Saviors go on in the delusion that their personal needs don't matter. They go on in the delusion that all that matters is the business of the kingdom, but they wrongly define the business of the kingdom as getting people saved and straightened up. Is this what Jesus died for? To get people into the church so they can tithe and lead respectable lives?

Jesus' heart absolutely breaks over the pain and loneliness in the lives of most Christians. He wants to love that pain away and chase out the fear (1 John 4:18), but we don't have time for him to do that in us. We have people to minister to! It fascinates me how unbiblical this is. What Scripture teaches instead is that God often takes a person and locks her away for years so he can love her and restore her to health. *Then* he sends her out to do his work. God wasn't in a hurry with Moses, John the Baptist or Paul. Each one of them spent years being rebuilt as a person before he was pressed into service. We, however, get 'em saved, get 'em equipped, and get 'em busy. Is this really God's way?

CONTROL FREAK

I said that the Savior lives her life as though her needs don't matter. In actuality, nobody can live that way. My needs and your needs do matter, and we will get them met somehow. We do it either honestly or dishonestly. But we do it. The Savior believes that his needs are irrelevant—and can quote the Scriptures to prove it. He may say, "Jesus first, others second and myself last," but, in actuality, his relational mask is deeply selfish and controlling.

As a recovering Savior, I know. Years ago, when I was very concerned about my wife's lack of spiritual growth, I would "encourage" her. When I came home from work, I would ask if she'd prayed and read her Bible. Understand, I wasn't pushy or self-righteous about it. I was sweet and kind in my delivery, but she always got angry (which hurt my feelings) and only confirmed to me all the more how "unspiritual" she was. My manipulation was obvious to everyone but me.

What I thought was pastoring her was actually pestering her. I couldn't understand why she didn't see my heart. I only wanted her to grow spiritually. What's wrong with that? This is when God began to show me that my definition of love was very self-serving. Yes, I wanted her to grow, but if I was honest, I had to admit that I wanted her to grow so that my needs could be met. You see, if she was walking with the Lord in power, then she would be loving, attentive and affirming of *me* too.

Sure, there was genuine concern about her growth mixed in, but there was a lot of selfishness there that I wasn't being honest about.

God also reminded me that he was at least as concerned about her spiritual growth as I was (duh!). If I wanted her to grow, maybe I should ask someone to influence her who could get past her defenses better than I. Furthermore, the Lord said to me, if I really wanted her to grow for *her* benefit (and not mine), I needed to let her work it out with him. Do you see how controlling Saviors really are? And all in the name of love or ministry.

Saviors' dominance doesn't end with their spouses; they control their kids, extended family and friends as well. Again, it's all done in the name of Jesus. We have only two weapons at our disposal for influencing others: love and guilt. Saviors use the weapon of guilt very skillfully. They don't mean to use guilt as a weapon; they just do. It's all they know. It's the weapon that's been used against them.

Here's an important principle that every Christian (Savior or not) needs to understand: *We always give to others what we think we are getting from God.* If I believe that God is motivating me through guilt or fear, that's what I'll use to motivate others. I will preach, nag and remind others of what they should be doing. If I feel an underlying "I'm not measuring up" in my own heart, then that's what I'll preach to those around me. I may do it sweetly and with the sincerest of hearts, but it's still control. And people usually resist control.

Jesus is so different from us. When the rich young ruler asked, "What must I do to inherit eternal life?" Jesus referred him to the commandments. "All these I have kept since I was a boy," the ruler lied (Mark 10:20). Then Jesus told him exactly what he needed to do: free himself from the materialism that ruled his life and become a disciple. The blood drained out of this young man's face, and he went away sad.

Here's the fascinating part: Jesus let him go. How could he do that? Didn't he care? Oh, he did, and he cared deeply: "Jesus looked at him and loved him" (Mark 10:21). The real Savior allows people to make

THINGS SAVIORS DO:

- keep themselves in a constant state of activity
- allow others to violate their boundaries
- have a strong "rescuing impulse"
- neglect their own needs
- work to exhaustion and then complain about it
- hide bitterness in their heart
- have their hand in a dozen ministries

their own decisions *even if they are wrong*. Jesus does this because he knows something about human nature that pseudo-Saviors don't: real growth and change happen only when they are freely chosen. But freedom of choice is something Saviors cannot abide.

If you watch and listen to them, you will see that they are trying to push others toward a certain objective. They do it through rewards and punishments. They do it through their sweetness or their hurt silence. They do it in ways that are obvious and in ways that no one (not even they) would guess. Their every gesture, tone and facial expression is an attempt to move others toward an envisioned goal for that individual.

Real growth and change happen only when they are freely chosen.

Saviors live by all the core beliefs previously described: *God can't be trusted; that's why he needs so much of my help. The Bible does not apply to me, at least when it addresses my own neediness or sins. I don't need other people, but they sure do need me. Romance or sex will meet my deepest needs; that's why I'm always telling my spouse how he or she can improve. If I am honest I will be abandoned; that's why I'll never acknowledge how lonely, needy or angry I am. I must do everything perfectly or I am worthless; that's why I have zero tolerance for failure—my own or anyone*

*else's. And intimate relationships bring only pain; that's why I'll serve you,
teach you and care for you, but I'll never let you into my soul.*

Saviors are usually some of the kindest and most moral people you
will ever meet. They don't smoke, drink, cuss or watch bad movies.
Their spirituality is obvious to everyone. Or is it? In reality, their basic
approach to life and relationships is obscenely controlling, and the
people closest to them resent it. But those in the outer circle are very
impressed with Saviors and may not discern their unhealthy behavior pattern.

WHAT IS A SAVIOR TO DO?

Saviors are very lonely people who are too scared to acknowledge the
depth of it to themselves or anyone else, but the way to deal with
loneliness is not to make yourself indispensable to those around you.
The way to deal with loneliness is to come to the One who alone understands and comforts the deepest needs of the human heart.

Here is where Saviors are at a distinct disadvantage. They don't believe that Jesus wants *primarily* to care for them; they believe he
wants them to care for others. Again, as spiritual as this sounds, it is
mistaken. Jesus came to give *you* life (John 10:10). He came to give
you rest (Psalm 23; Isaiah 30:15; Matthew 11:28-30). He came to
quench *your* thirst (Isaiah 55:1-3; John 4:14; 7:37). He told the disciples that his "food" was to do the will of the Father and to finish his
work (John 4:34). He said this just after he'd loved the Samaritan
woman and given her hope for the first time in her dreary life. The
Father's "will and work" for Jesus was for him to love and heal his
broken sons and daughters. He didn't come from heaven just to re-
cruit project managers; he came to love you.

Of course, when we do get loved by Jesus, we are eager to touch
other people. This is the secret to real ministry, but most of us (especially Saviors) don't operate this way. We minister, care for others and

help in an unconscious attempt to find love and security. This is exactly opposite the ministry and model our Lord gave us. Prior to washing the disciples' feet, "Jesus knew that the Father had put all things under his power, and that he had come from God and was returning to God; so he got up, . . . wrapped a towel around his waist, . . . poured water into a basin and began to wash his disciples' feet" (John 13:3-5).

Notice that before Jesus did anything *he knew who he was*. He didn't perform this humble act in order to show the disciples his meekness. Nor did he do it to establish or reinforce his own spirituality or godliness. He already had a clear knowledge of who he was, where he'd come from and where he was going before he did anything for anybody. Do you see how different this is from the motivation behind most of our ministry activities?

Before Jesus did anything *he knew who he was.*

For years I lived in this very place. I was always wondering who I was or what God was calling me to do. Understand, there is nothing wrong with this. In fact, young adults all wonder about this. It is appropriate at that age, but my never-ending search for significance drove much of what I did in ministry.

When I was able to teach or preach, I felt very validated. When I could help around the church or buy some homeless person a meal, I felt good. But it wouldn't be long before my nagging self-doubts returned and I began obsessing on "What does God want for my life?" When someone else was picked to teach the class or lead the outreach, I experienced depression. This was a dead giveaway to my core belief that I had worth only if I was a recognized Christian leader.

God used me in some powerful ways, but much of my service for him and others was driven by an urgency to find myself through ministry. God had to strip me of this shame-based drive and teach me how to find my worth exclusively in him. In fact, I'm still learning this lesson. My tendency to find my worth and value in an idolatrous source (even ministry) still confronts me regularly.

It's normal to crave validation from others, but Saviors find their sense of self almost exclusively in the praise and admiration of those they help. They will say they do it for God, which is partly true, but the majority of their service is an unconscious search for human affirmation. But, "how can you believe if you accept praise from one another, yet make no effort to obtain the praise that comes from the only God?" (John 5:44).

Unless we allow Jesus to serve us, we cannot join him in his service to others (see John 13:6-9). It is only when he serves us that we have anything to offer. The smartest thing anyone can do if he wants to "serve God" is to sit at God's feet on a regular basis and soak up all his love and affection (see Luke 10:39, 42). As backwards as it sounds, we have to learn how to luxuriate in God's love for us—not try harder to love him: "This is love: not that we loved God, but that he loved us and sent his Son as an atoning sacrifice for our sins" (1 John 4:10). As we do this we have something to offer back to God and others.

SAVIORS REDEEMED

Saviors excel at demonstrating mercy. The problem is that they don't turn it inward. What if Saviors took their skill at showing mercy and aimed it at themselves? What if they allowed themselves imperfection without carrying around all the condemnation that goes with it? What if Saviors allowed others in the body of Christ to minister exclusively to them? These are big challenges for Saviors, and we've shown the reason why: there is a root of shame that has told them all their life that others are worth focusing on but *they* aren't.

The Savior redeemed is a remarkable sight. Gone are the perfectionism and pride that say they don't need anyone to help them. Gone is the need always to be the benevolent giver and never the grateful receiver. Gone is the hidden sin of superiority that causes them to see themselves as sinners, yes, but not as bad as the rest. Gone is their coming to God only to receive the next assignment.

Saviors who can allow themselves to bask in their own gift of mercy are beautiful people indeed. They will never lose their gracious touch. In fact, it will deepen and become even more fruitful. When Saviors can give ministry to others (as they always have) but *receive* it as well, there will finally be equality in the body of Christ (see 1 Corinthians 12:25). When Saviors discard their messianic robes, then the true Savior can work in them and through them as never before.

TIPS FOR SAVIORS

- Pray and study, not to show God how "serious" you are but to bask in his love.
- When others come to you seeking help for something they should do on their own, learn the power of the word *no*.
- Stop feeling guilty for taking care of your own needs.
- Don't carry the world on your shoulders. (Only one Person has shoulders that broad.)
- Don't obsess over all the bad things that bad people do (Psalm 37:1). Realize this is human nature and you have very limited power to stop it.
- Seek relationships where you can drop your titles and soak up the love of others.
- Eat healthfully, exercise and do "unspiritual" (but not sinful)

things, simply because they are fun.

- Read Scripture and Christian books for your own enrichment with no thought of how you can teach it to others.
- If you've lost your sense of humor, get it back.
- Become childlike.
- Abandon your causes and try to love both your friends and your enemies.
- Don't strive to be adult, respectable or socially acceptable to the Christians around you. Strive to be honest.
- Learn what Matthew 11:28-30 means and practice it often.

THE AGGRESSOR

Hostility as a Shield

William pastored a large church and was an evangelistic dynamo. He was also an effective fundraiser. I was delighted when he offered to help me and my small parachurch ministry. I had heard from other leaders that William was "the master" when it came to getting things done and paying for them. Indeed he was.

I met with William at his church, and he showed me how to write fundraising letters that were direct and to the point. He gave me very practical advice about how to strengthen the financial base of our ministry and nurture our donors. I was very grateful for his personal interest in me and our work. It was paying off.

I did grow increasingly uncomfortable, however, with William's insistence that I *tell* donors to give and not ask. Asking left them "an out," he said. He reminded me that he had studied all of the effective fundraising strategies and that his large ministry was proof that they worked. I couldn't argue with that, but something was still troubling me.

I spent an entire morning praying and poring over the Scriptures, looking for guidance. Second Corinthians 6-9 showed me how to raise funds in a way that was pure, kind and truthful. I was told not to exploit people or put them under compulsion. These words jumped off the page and put in writing what I was feeling inside. I knew what I had to do. I called William and set up an appointment to talk about my concerns. I wanted to do it in person.

I knew not only that William was a dynamic leader but also that he didn't like it when people disagreed with him. I'd heard some horror stories. I knew that my chances of getting blasted were pretty high, but I wanted to be honest.

William was very warm when I stepped into his office a few days later. I began by telling him how much I appreciated his help and the practical guidance he'd given me. I told him I did have a concern, however, with an approach to fundraising that seemed a little coercive. I shared my heart in an open and respectful way. Apparently it still sounded like an attack.

"Are you saying that I'm manipulative?" he shouted.

"I'm saying that I'm uncomfortable with the approach you're telling me I have to take if I want your ongoing help."

"Well, you don't have to *worry* about that!" he roared. "You obviously don't want my help. Go and do it yourself."

"That's not what I'm saying, William. I *do* want your help and the financial support that you and the church have given us. But can't we disagree on this point, or do I have to do it exactly as you're telling me?"

"No, we can't," he said. "Because you're telling me that I'm lying, cheating and manipulating people, and you don't want to do what I do."

I told William that I didn't believe he was "a liar" or "a cheat"; I just wanted the freedom to raise funds in a way that wasn't so forceful. I told him that I felt I could be direct and yet respectful at the same time. By this point he couldn't even hear me. He was pounding his desk with his fist and using profanity. He even began to cry. "I get so *angry* when people do this!" he said.

I wondered what was really going on here. Who had hurt this man so deeply that even a kind presentation of brotherly disagreement was seen as a frontal assault on his dignity? He had a few more things to say about me wanting to rule my own little kingdom and not wanting to grow into a large, effective ministry. I didn't want to stick around for any more, but I chose to stay and be completely present.

"William, if I'm wrong, I'm eager for the Lord to show me that. And I will be the first one to laugh with you."

William wasn't laughing. He got out from behind his desk and put his hand on my shoulder. I felt pushed in the direction of the door and knew we were done. "Well, God *bless* you!" he said, as he patted me on the back so hard I almost stumbled.

I walked out to my car and just sat there for a while. "Lord, I haven't been spiritually abused like that in twenty years. It would be easy right now for me to write this man off, but I acknowledge that you've used William powerfully in this town. I won't give in to the temptation to demonize him, in spite of the appalling treatment I just received."

That day William informed his secretary that the church's relationship with New Creation Ministries was terminated and all financial contributions were to be stopped. It's not fun being on the wrong side of an Aggressor.

MEANNESS AND FEARFULNESS

The Aggressors of the world—how can I say this?—just seem to be jerks. Their behavior would certainly qualify them for that title. But Aggressors are not what they seem. Wherever you find anger, you find fear. As cocky, pushy or I-don't-give-a-rip-about-what-people-think as Aggressors might appear, they are ruled by fear.

Aggressors have been deeply hurt and/or abandoned by key people in their lives and are stuck in the anger stage of the grieving process. Behind every threatening Aggressor you will find a wounded little boy or girl. Janelle is an example. Her husband, Michael, had an affair that brought the two of them into my office. Michael was sorry for what he'd done and acknowledged that he'd hurt Janelle deeply.

Janelle didn't flinch. "D____ right I'm hurt! You *lied* to me, and I will never be able to trust you again!"

Michael shook his head in a way that said, "You have every right to feel that way."

Apart from his infidelity, Michael was a passive man who never offended anybody (remember the Avoider?). He had a Ph.D. in people-pleasing. He tried to get along with everybody and succeeded fairly well, but when it came to his wife, he could do no right. Janelle was always picking at something. If it wasn't the way he dressed or the way he talked, she was picking on

> **YOU MIGHT BE AN AGGRESSOR IF**
>
> - you *can't stand* people who don't take action
> - you are wildly successful in ministry or business
> - you have a scary temper
> - you have lots of opinions and you're not afraid to share them
> - you have lots of arguments with people
> - even when you relax, you run yourself ragged
> - you believe ministry is more important than worship

him about how "he never stood up to anybody." After ten years of this he decided to stand up to her in the only way he knew, a secret, passive-aggressive way: have a relationship with someone else.

I never for a moment told Michael or Janelle that this justified his affair. I called it sin and I called it damnably selfish, but Michael was reacting to *something*. Janelle had always had this edge to her personality. As the song says, she was "cold as ice." As a mortgage broker she mixed very well with her clients and colleagues, but everyone knew Janelle didn't take any bull. If she believed something, she was not afraid to say it, and if she thought you were an idiot, she would tell you.

Not only did she make money hand over fist, she also was sought out by people in her church. If a retreat needed planning or an event needed organizing, Janelle was your woman. She was great at getting things accomplished and delegating responsibilities to others. If she was at the head of a project, it was as good as done.

But Janelle had no idea how to be intimate. She could control people, but she could not connect with them (her husband or anyone else). Janelle's father was a very quiet man who rarely spoke. He probably suffered from major depression but refused to get treatment. When she spoke with her dad, he would barely grunt, even in his old age. Each time this happened, Janelle felt like a worthless human being all over again.

From childhood she determined two things: first, she would never again allow herself to need anyone; and second, she would do everything herself and plow over anyone who stood in her path. She was famous for saying things like "Lead, follow or get out of the way."

Michael worked very hard to change his passive, people-pleasing ways. His wife would tell me, "Yes, he's making improvements, but he still doesn't do such and such." If he helped around the house, he didn't do it right. If he tried to reel in their rebellious son, he was too soft. If he got one thing right, he failed at five.

At first I encouraged Michael to jump through as many hoops as he could. I reminded him that the burden for change was on his shoulders; but after six months, Janelle's anger about the affair had not lessened. I knew this was bigger than the affair. She refused even to consider that maybe there was sin on her part. Her husband's adultery was unconscionable, but her never-ending contempt for him seemed perfectly justified in her mind.

When I pointed out that it wasn't just Michael she felt this way about, she always had an excuse: "Well, I do that to my coworker because he's a jerk too," or "I said that to the choir director because she had no right to do what she did." And so it went.

The turning point came a year after I began seeing them. One Saturday morning Michael was relaxing on the couch in his stocking feet. Janelle walked by and said, "Get your feet off that couch right now!" The years of frustration and abuse, coupled with the fact that he was being told he couldn't put his feet on a couch that he himself owned, caused something to snap. Michael sprang off the sofa and was right in his wife's face. His crazed look caught her totally by surprise. Michael saw himself hitting her with all his strength, but all he actually did was stand in front of her and quiver with rage.

Janelle backed down for the first time in eleven years. She saw a lifetime of hateful treatment reflected back to her in a moment's time. She was stunned and depressed. Michael, however, felt strangely empowered and free. Now he was the one feeling justified in his anger. Janelle had finally succeeded in changing him.

IN SLAVERY TO FEAR

Such tragedies are played out in Christian marriages every day. We can certainly lay blame on pornography, workaholism or a dozen other factors. But the common theme I've seen in every conflicted marriage I've ever dealt with is this: one or two people with a relational mask they refuse to repent of.

To Aggressors, life is a threatening experience requiring constant suspicion and guardedness. Naturally it isn't long before the world "proves" their basic hypothesis. In reality, the fearful and angry lenses through which they look blind them to the beauty and love that could be theirs. Their life becomes a self-fulfilling prophecy.

Why is it so hard for Aggressors to let go of their self-protective armor? Because anger is not their biggest problem—fear is. The writer of Hebrews tells us that at the cross Jesus destroyed the one who holds the power of death, that is, the devil. By this power Satan has been able to keep us in slavery all our lives to our fear of death (Hebrews 2:14-15).

Obviously this "fear of death" refers to our unspoken dread of physical death and the hell that follows. But if that's all we take from the verse, we are missing something crucial. How many men and women walk around saying, "I'm so afraid of dying and going to hell"? Do we see them living their lives in such a way as to alert us to this secret fear? No, but we *do* see men and women living their lives in such a way as to protect themselves from the thing they fear most: abandonment.

Anger is not the Aggressor's biggest problem—fear is.

Avoiders act out their fear by running at the first sign of trouble. Aggressors act out theirs by rejecting others before they can be rejected themselves. Because of their lifelong slavery to fear of abandonment, Aggressors abandon others preemptively. Sadly they've done this so long they don't even see it anymore. Many of their words, gestures and attitudes say, "Don't get too close. I bite!"

Many Aggressors also have a giant fear of being seen as weak. That's why they need the gruff or no-nonsense exterior. To them weakness is the same as being stupid or pathetic. Aggressors are hateful and full of contempt for those they perceive as weak. And they hate and fear it in themselves (because they know deep down it is there), but fear of being seen as weak is still fear of abandonment, just one step removed.

The Aggressor husband is greatly surprised when his wife won't have sex with him. In his feelings of being abandoned, he lashes out again, causing her to back away further. The Aggressor wife is hurt that her husband won't spend time with her and tells him directly that he is a failure. Predictably he puts as much distance as he can between them.

Is there no hope for such bound-up women and men? There is, but it involves the hardest work of all. It requires that they repent, not just of specific words or deeds, but also of their *orientation*. This is why I get angry when Christians focus so much on how homosexuals need to repent—not because I disagree but because our God commands *each of us* to repent of our deep-seated and seemingly invincible orientations.

To repent of something so etched into the fiber of our beings will require nothing less than a desperate, moment-by-moment clinging to Jesus Christ. This is what discipleship looks like. Always has. Nevertheless, millions of us will enter heaven with our relational masks intact. Thankfully God won't reject us because of our refusal to engage this problem, but the missed opportunities on earth will be staggering.

Apparently many of us are content to let our old nature wreak havoc on the people around us as long as we "make it to heaven." The Scriptures are clear that many saved people will stand before God only to see the fire burn up what they thought was a commendable life (1 Corinthians 3:12-15). They themselves will be saved, but they will be stunned by their attitudes, motives and personality traits that went unchecked on earth. None of us has to wait until then for our life to be "revealed by fire." We can have the Holy Spirit pour his fire on us now and judge everything that is not of him (Matthew 3:11-12).

PAUL, THE RECOVERING AGGRESSOR

Do we have an example in Scripture of a person like this coming into health? We do, and his name is Paul. In Paul we have a clear picture of what is needed for someone ruled by fear and rage to be changed. We all know the key points of Paul's story: persecutor of the church, transformed on the Damascus road, shaped into the most powerful evangelist and Christian teacher of all time. Paul himself said that his transformation was a prototype for all the world to see (1 Timothy 1:16).

Prior to his conversion Paul (or Saul) was a very dangerous Aggressor. This is apparent in his murderous treatment of the first Christians (see Acts 7:55—8:3; 9:1-2; 22:4-5, 19-20; 26:9-11; Galatians 1:13), but if we stop there we will assume that the only real Aggressors are murderers or obvious abusers. Yet his treatment of others was actually fueled by a deeper aggression, which showed itself as legalism. This legalism was behind Saul's relentless ambition to be the greatest Jew of all time (Acts 26:4-5; Galatians 1:14).

THINGS AGGRESSORS SAY:

"Lead, follow or get out of the way!"

"Rest is for the weak."

"If you don't do it, I will!"

"I don't care what you think, this is the truth!"

"We were saved to serve."

"I know what I'm doing."

"I'm going to make these kids obey."

Outwardly legalists may appear to be the godliest people in the room. They are the most passionate and seem to be more sold out to Jesus than anybody else. They may win more souls and build more churches, but is this really driven by the Holy Spirit, or is it driven by a fear of not being accepted by God? When people are motivated by a fear of rejection, they often compensate by outworking everyone around them. This protects them, they think, from ever being rejected. Their tireless and "superior" work ethic puts them in a class that is seemingly beyond criticism.

Saul excelled in this. His passion "for God" drove him to study harder, pray longer and hate more deeply than the ordinary Jews around him. If anyone had suggested to the young Pharisee that his ambition was powered by anything but God, he would have been deeply offended. This defensiveness and anger were a dead giveaway of Saul's fear.

What does Saul's preconversion legalism have to do with us? If you are a Christian Aggressor, everything! Are you positive that your tire-less work on the committee, your time in the Sunday school or your zeal for doctrinal correctness are motivated by God? If you are sure the answer is yes, how do you think the Mormon, Muslim or Jeho-vah's Witness would answer the same question? If you are an Aggres-sor, I encourage you to let the Holy Spirit do some sifting. Religious zeal—even of the evangelical type—can have a source other than God. You can learn that now or you can learn it in another world.

THE AGGRESSOR CORRALLED

After the shock of the Damascus road experience, what did Jesus do to heal this recovering Aggressor? He took Paul out of circulation. This is so key that we could easily devote an entire book to the sub-ject. Indeed many writers over the centuries have done exactly that, but we haven't listened to them. We still don't. The church is full of Aggressors—uh, I mean ambitious men and women advancing the kingdom of God. Like Saviors, their motto is, "Get 'em saved, get 'em trained, and get 'em busy!" Though prevalent, this approach to rais-ing up Christians is completely off center.

When God got ahold of Paul, the first thing he did was spirit him away from all ministry, service to others or "advancement of the king-dom." A cursory reading of Acts 9 indicates that Paul was confronted on the road by the Lord, received ministry from Ananias and then jumped right into evangelistic work in Damascus (see Acts 9:1-25). But Paul clarifies this for us in Galatians: "I did not consult any man, nor did I go up to Jerusalem to see those who were apostles before I was, but I went immediately into Arabia and *later* returned to Damas-cus. Then after three years, I went up to Jerusalem" (Galatians 1:16-18, emphasis added).

Though the chronology isn't completely clear, one thing is certain: Paul spent anywhere from a few months to a few years in solitude before he jumped into the thick of things. This is the first thing God does to every Aggressor: he takes him or her out of circulation so he can show them what is really important. This shouldn't be a surprise to anyone who's read the Bible. God did the same thing with Abraham, Moses, the prophets, John the Baptist and others.

If this is typical of God's dealings with his servants, then it is doubly crucial for Aggressors to submit to this discipline, but alas, they usually don't. Their aggressive nature and the support of an enabling church or ministry usually fast-tracks them into ministry as soon as possible.

Yes, God often uses Aggressors and blesses their lives, but this can only go so far. Eventually their missed appointments with solitude will catch up to them, and they will keep their reservation at the Desert Inn. They always crash, burn, fry or sin. Then they are ready to go back to where they left off: the place wise men and women of the past *started*—the place of secret prayer, submission to a wise mentor or years-long character development. Whatever we want to call it, they eventually find their way back to the starting place. This is where the dismantling of the Aggressor relational mask begins.

THE AGGRESSOR BROKEN

What happened to Paul in the Arabian Desert? We don't really know, but we do know this: he went through a process not unlike his predecessors'; he was forced to be quiet, unproductive and focused on restoration. Moses tended sheep; Paul made tents. David lived in the desert beyond the reach of Saul and got to know God; Paul lived in the desert beyond the reach of "busyness" and got to know Jesus. The prophets met God in the wilderness and were changed; so also Paul. Like Paul, every one of us has to unlearn the stuff we think we know and be reeducated by the Holy Spirit.

I can imagine Paul quietly working at his business and spending hours alone with the Lord during this time. He wasn't leading Bible studies or doing miracles; he was letting the Great Physician heal him of years of legalism, shame and naked ambition. Paul came to see the damage his aggression had done. He wasn't about to do something else "for God" until he knew it was time.

As I said, most of us don't submit to this in the beginning but come back to it later. Such was the case with Catherine. Catherine worked as a substitute teacher, supervised the Christian education department at her large church and was on the board of the women's ministry there. She and her husband came to me because their relationship was basically platonic.

When people are cut off from those closest to them, it is a dead giveaway about their relationship with God (regardless of how "successful" their ministry is). When I began to speak with Catherine about this, she was resistant. Over time she realized that she was indeed cut off from God and from her spouse as well. I told her she couldn't be teacher of the year or ministry person of the decade and still have time left over for intimacy with God and her spouse.

> **When people are cut off from those
> closest to them, it is a dead giveaway about
> their relationship with God.**

She admitted that I was only telling her what she already suspected. In Catherine's case, radical surgery was needed. She and her husband agreed that she needed to quit her job. They had to sell the boat and downsize a bit, but she and her family were the better for it. She also realized that she needed to get out of ministry. Her pastor was in full agreement. He appreciated Catherine's gifts but had become increasingly concerned about her hectic life.

Catherine and her husband plugged into a couples' group that kept them accountable for their relationship. The two of them got refocused on their relationships to God, each other and the kids. The transition took about six months, but they've never been happier. Catherine is slowly and carefully starting her own business now. Minus the workaholism. She's told me she'll be involved in formal ministry only when she can do it in a healthy way.

> **THINGS AGGRESSORS DO:**
>
> • "speak the truth" no matter who gets hurt
>
> • excel in work but fail at rest
>
> • keep themselves on the go
>
> • offend others by their attitude
>
> • always see themselves as right
>
> • use the Bible to clobber others
>
> • believe anyone who disagrees with them is the enemy
>
> • drive people away and then complain about how lonely they are

THE AGGRESSOR TAMED

Both Paul and Catherine learned to submit their aggressive tendencies to Jesus. Paul wasn't "cured," however. On at least a few occasions, the old aggression came out, and he had to bring it back under the authority of Jesus (see Acts 15:37-39; 23:1-5). For the Aggressor, the answer is not to become passive but to be tamed.

A strong, muscular horse would be useless if his spirit was completely broken. All that raw power has to be channeled and directed. The end result is a mighty stallion obeying its master's every command. That's what God wants to do with every Aggressor, but they have to submit to his training. For me that training involved being called into the ministry when I was eighteen, only to be broken, busted and groomed for the next thirteen years. I labored in obscurity as a construction worker and taught occasional Bible studies until I was ready to step into my God-given purpose at age thirty-one.

I will be the first to say that I *hated* that time in my life. I thought God had forgotten about me or that I'd made up all the promises I thought I'd heard from him in my youth. I was wrong on both counts. God took a young man who needed to accomplish great things in order to find his worth and showed him how to find his worth exclusively in Jesus. He showed me how broken I was, how wrong my definition of ministry was and how driven I was by my own agenda.

Every one of these lessons came with the force of a lash. While my friends went to Bible college and then on to ministry, God was roughing me up behind the shed. It didn't seem fair. I've lived long enough, however, to see some of those same friends lose their ministries, marriages and integrity. For me, this has not been an occasion for gloating but for warning. I am so glad now that I let God beat the stuffing out of me at the beginning rather than forcing him to do it later (after I'd done all my damage).

If you are an Aggressor who hasn't submitted to God's program of solitude, quietness and obscurity (and you see the tragic results), don't despair. Yes, you may have hurt other people or done some damage you can't repair, but God isn't done with you. He wants to heal you and give you purpose. He wants to give you value and worth in your *relationship with him,* not in what you do.

Paul understood that God had a calling on his life from the beginning (Galatians 1:15; Romans 11:29), even though he had botched it so badly. Thankfully he submitted to God's new program of grace wherein he takes controlling, obsessive women and men and changes them into disciplined soldiers of Christ. Hear Paul's final word on this: "But for that very reason I was shown mercy so that in me, the worst of sinners, Christ Jesus might display his unlimited patience as an example for those who would believe on him and receive eternal life" (1 Timothy 1:16).

THE AGGRESSOR REDEEMED

God isn't calling every Aggressor to become as quiet as a mouse. He is calling every Aggressor to focus the mighty power of aggression in the right way. You may notice that I've used the example of the horse. The horse is caught, corralled, broken and then tamed. If the powerful horse becomes docile and simply lies down, then we've lost everything. God does not have a problem with you having a strong personality. He's given you that trait, but sin wants to capture it and use it to destroy you and those around you. This you must not permit.

By nature, Aggressors actually have something that others don't: an innate ability to bring all their mental and emotional energy to bear on a problem. What happens when Aggressors learn to direct their energy instead of being dragged around by their own aggressiveness? What happens when an Aggressor repents and says, "God, whatever you give me to do I will do with all my might, but I will go no further than you tell me"? Paul, such a great example of this, wrote, "We, however, will not boast beyond proper limits, but will confine our boasting to the field God has assigned to us" (2 Corinthians 10:13).

The unhealed Aggressor habitually tramples all over people—going way past proper limits. But the Aggressor who is learning to let Jesus have his way in her heart is able to be quiet and reserved. She doesn't have to make everyone do or think what she says. That same person is also able to spring into action at a moment's notice when the Holy Spirit or the situation demands it.

The man or woman who lives out of the brokenness of the Aggressor is like a dam that bursts and sweeps away everything in its path. The person who channels his aggressive nature and brings it under his own control (with the help of God's Spirit and God's people) is like a powerful river that stays within its banks, nourishing everything in its path.

God needs people who can jump in and do what other men and women can't. When he commands you to act, you can open it up and fly down the highway. But when the time for forceful action is over, you will have the power to be gentle and self-effacing. Instead of scorching everyone in your path, you will now be able to contain your hot flame to the hearth where everyone can be warmed and comforted.

TIPS FOR AGGRESSORS

- Don't apologize for the power God has given you; just be sure not to misuse it.

- Loving people is more important than "getting things done." Never forget that.

- Don't lose hope if God puts you on the bench for a long time. If you continue submitting to him, you *will* be sent into the game and you *will* conquer.

- You will think you are ready long before God does.

- God doesn't want you to become an Avoider or a Savior, but you can learn something important from both.

- Might doesn't make right, and heat doesn't equal light.

- Understand how your Aggressive relational mask isolates you from intimacy, and aggressively work to change it.

- Be aggressive about treating people justly, showing mercy and being humble (Micah 6:8).

- Find out if someone really wants or needs what you are offering before you give it to him.

- Find out what boundaries are. The person stuck in the negative aspects of the Aggressor has no clue.

- Be aggressive in throwing wide the doors of your heart to the loving, healing presence of Jesus (Matthew 11:12).

- Those who are privately aggressive in their intimacy with God are a public blessing.

8
THE SPIRITUALIZER

God as a Mask

Rhonda was hard to get close to. It almost seemed she feared her face would crack if she smiled too much. And that was too bad, because it was a pretty one. When I talked with her by herself, she would tell me all the things God was saying to her. She also told me how heavy her "burden" was for her husband. Without a doubt, Rhonda had a genuine relationship with Jesus. But, frankly, I think she was even too spiritual for him!

Her husband, Doug, agreed: "Russell, I love my wife, but I feel like she's unapproachable. No matter what we're talking about, she always brings it back to the Bible."

Rhonda jumped right in. "See, that's the problem, Russell. Doug isn't walking closely with the Lord, so he doesn't want to talk about the Word with me."

Doug retorted, "How do *you* know how I'm doing with the Lord? Do you see me when I pray or read? Do you know the conversations that he and I have?"

"Well, I sure don't see evidence of it at home," Rhonda replied.

"That's because I use my lunch hour to connect with God. I just don't advertise it like you do."

At that Rhonda got a hurt look on her face and turned away slightly. Doug was quick to apologize. "Honey, I'm sorry. I'm not trying to hurt your feelings. It just seems to me that every time I try to get close you bring up some failure in my life and tell me what I should do about it."

"Somebody has to!" she said.

As I looked at these two, my heart ached for both of them. For Doug because I saw him sticking his neck out and trying to express his feelings but being judged each time he did. For Rhonda because I knew something was going on inside her. Something was causing her to keep a religious distance between herself and others.

Doug was a really decent guy who worked hard to support Rhonda and their three kids. He was a great dad (Rhonda agreed) and was not afraid to help around the house. But he smoked, and that made Rhonda very uneasy. Not only that but, according to Rhonda, he liked his sports "too much."

A WOMAN IN PAIN

In the weeks that followed, Rhonda and I discussed her past. One day it came to light that she'd been raised by an alcoholic mother who was totally out of control. She assured me, however, that the Lord had healed all those wounds. She told me about her mother's boyfriends and the hell that she and her little brother lived through. It sounded awful.

"How do you feel when you think about that?" I asked her.

"I don't feel anything about it. I just wish my mom would come to the Lord," she said.

As I asked more and more questions, it became harder for Rhonda to track with me. She would give me vague answers like, "That's in the Lord's hands" or "I'm just trusting him about that." But when I asked her what "trust" meant, she couldn't give me anything concrete. She would quote a verse and tell me she was trying to obey that.

"As you obey that verse, what does it look like for you?" I would ask. It was hard for her to give me a straight answer. It became obvious that she was just reciting Scripture but not necessarily understanding it or working out its painful details.

Rhonda's teens were a very hard time, and her mom didn't make things any easier. It seems the only one who could feel anger or hurt in the family was the mother. Rhonda and her brother were not allowed to express their feelings (unless those feelings were in line with Mom's).

At fourteen Rhonda found the Lord. Finally she had someone who would love her and understand her, she said. She dived into the life of her youth group and church. Her mom wasn't real happy about her "hanging out with those fanatics," but she tolerated it. Rhonda organized prayer for her mom and set about to lead her to Christ. Mom wasn't interested.

Rhonda found comfort in reading her Bible, listening to Christian music and immersing herself in all things evangelical. In no time she was speaking the lingo and rose to a position of leadership in her youth group. One thing Rhonda didn't do, however, was feel her feelings. She became convinced that feelings were more of a nuisance than anything else. In place of honest emotions, a rigid theology began to form. Out of the ashes of her chaotic family she began to carve a life that was orderly and predictable.

I couldn't escape the feeling that Rhonda was living in a cage, but how could I tell her that? She would think I was attacking her relationship with God, but I gave it a try. I told her that I appreciated her heart for God (and I did) but that it seemed there was more healing Jesus needed to do. When I suggested that there might still be pain regarding her mother, she got angry.

"Why do you keep bringing that up!" she almost yelled. "I am *so* over that."

"Then why do you look like you're about to cry?" I asked.

You can guess what happened next.

Getting honest about her pain really messed up Rhonda's religion. She wasn't nearly as sure of everything as she had been before. I assured her that I wasn't trying to lead her away from the Lord or his Word—but closer. Slowly I helped her see that she had used Jesus as a shield to keep people away. When she was fourteen, I pointed out, she had good reason to create distance between herself and some of the people in her life who were hurting her.

Instead of letting Jesus love her back to wholeness, Rhonda had used him to ward off anybody who tried to get too close. I told her she used her theology to keep even Jesus at bay. She was starting to get it. After that day she began putting away her formula prayers. She learned how to tell God what she was really feeling. She needed lots of reassurance from me that this "really was biblical." I was happy to provide that. The Psalms were especially helpful. We talked a lot about grace (a major sticking point for Spiritualizers). She became increasingly human right before my eyes.

NO EASY STEREOTYPES

Rhonda is just one of several types of Spiritualizers. There are others. Sadly the women and men who wrap this re-

---

YOU MIGHT BE A SPIRITUALIZER IF

- you see Christians with different beliefs or practices as less spiritual than you

- in your mind, all problems can be solved with a Bible verse or a quote from Christian literature

- you have strong feelings about the right translation, the right spiritual leader or the right denomination

- you are deeply offended when anyone tries to point out a fault

- you are uncomfortable around non-Christians

- it is crucial to you that others see the wisdom of your beliefs

- you believe that emotions get in the way of spirituality

- you hunger to be recognized as a spiritual person

- you are puzzled by the recurring problems in your marriage or family

lational mask around their hearts don't even know it. Of course, this is true of all the relational masks. That's why they're so hard to spot in ourselves. Paul gives us an insightful list of Spiritualizers in 1 Corinthians 13. We all know this famous chapter, but most of us don't see the relevance of his list to our own lives. Let's look at the unique forms that Spiritualizers take according to Paul.

The Powerful Spiritualizer. In verse one of 1 Corinthians 13, Paul talks about those who hide behind the gifts of the Spirit: "If I speak in the tongues of men and of angels, but have not love, I am only a resounding gong or a clanging cymbal." Many followers of Jesus pride themselves on the fact that they speak in tongues, prophesy or believe in miracles. This can easily become another layer in the wrapping of the Spiritualizer.

Let me be clear—I have nothing against the gifts of the Spirit. I've been a charismatic for more than twenty years, and I believe in the practice of all the gifts. But I do have something against dishonesty. The man who prays in his spiritual language and then verbally cuts his children to pieces is not a spiritual man. He is a man who is not looking closely at the wounds or anger in his own soul. Likewise, it doesn't matter how stirring a woman's prophecies are if she is blind to what the Spirit is trying to show her about her own sin and brokenness.

You cannot really love anyone without being honest and knowing yourself.

I realize that everyone has growing to do. It's normal for inexperienced believers to run around "ministering" to everyone without seeing the immaturity in their own hearts. One hopes they will grow over the years so they can practice spiritual gifts *and* be authentic. You cannot really love anyone without being honest and knowing yourself. Hiding behind your "anointing" just won't do. God doesn't buy it and neither do a lot of others. It is cowardice in the Holy Spirit's name.

The Insightful Spiritualizer. In verse two Paul tells us that many who interact by means of this relating style have an intellectual bent to them: "If I can fathom all mysteries and all knowledge . . . but have not love, I am nothing." The Insightful Spiritualizer may be uncomfortable with the Holy Spirit stuff. Theological knowledge is his forte. This is the easiest type of spiritualizing to hide behind. We all know someone who can run intellectual circles around us and quote chapter and verse. Have you noticed that the people who relate this way can be downright judgmental of anyone who deviates in even the slightest degree from their theology?

The Insightful Spiritualizer will tell you he's only exercising "discernment." What's really happening is someone is believing something or experiencing something that makes him nervous, so it *must* be wrong. If it is flaws or errors in thinking that he's looking for, he doesn't have to look far, of course. The people around him give him an abundance of these to choose from. He pounces on those who advocate false doctrine or those caught up in questionable spiritual experience, but he is blind to his cold and loveless treatment of others. Being loving is not what counts for the Insightful Spiritualizer. Being right is what counts.

These people especially have to be right about God, because once they have the inside track on orthodoxy, nobody can touch them. To oppose them is to oppose God, so to speak. So you are guaranteed to lose if you tangle with them and God.

The Pedigreed Spiritualizer. There is a subcategory of Insightful Spiritualizer: the Pedigreed Spiritualizer. These are the people who not only know the truth about God but also know the truth about God's organization. They are superior to you because they have had the good sense to find the "true" body of Christ. They can trace their spiritual lineage back to Wesley, Calvin or the Pope. Or they sat under so-and-so's ministry (so they've *got* to be orthodox). Many see this for the smokescreen it is.

Certainly we have a right to be proud of our respective Christian traditions, but Pedigreed Spiritualizers secretly believe that their association with a certain body, movement or theology automatically marks them for superiority. This is no different from the Democrat or Republican who sees himself as excellent due to his alignment with the right party.

Paul destroys this way of finding security for ourselves: "Neither circumcision nor uncircumcision means anything; what counts is a new creation" (Galatians 6:15). The fact that I can prove that what I do goes all the way back to the early church fathers or reformers doesn't mean a thing. The real question is, Am I throwing off my insecure relational mask and living as a new creation? Am I trusting in a conversion formula or an institutional covering, or am I living in newness of life *today*? Insightful Spiritualizers trust in their knowledge of the right stuff. Pedigreed Spiritualizers trust in their practice of the right traditions.

The Revolutionary Spiritualizer. Some believers have an incredible heart for social causes and human suffering, but this too (according to Paul) can be a smokescreen for a loveless heart: "If I give all I possess to the poor . . . but have not love, I gain nothing" (1 Corinthians 13:3). Revolutionary Spiritualizers are the ones who take pride in championing the right cause. They have to be okay with God because they are prolife or working with the poor. Nobody would dare question their spirituality, because they feed the hungry, help the homeless or counsel runaways.

Revolutionary Spiritualizers see themselves on the cutting edge. In their mind the average Christian doesn't have the guts to do what they do. The only people who really love the Lord are those involved in urban ministry, missions or some other unpopular cause. Revolutionary Spiritualizers wrap their insecurity in a layer of sociopolitical elitism.

From a biblical standpoint, nothing is wrong with these causes or efforts. The Scriptures have much to say about caring for the poor and loving the broken. In fact, it is an indication of where we are with God: "If anyone has material possessions and sees his brother in need but has no pity on him, how can the love of God be in him? Dear children, let us not love with words or tongue but with actions and in truth" (1 John 3:17-18).

Every Christian should touch the needy in some way, just as every Christian should experience God's power, have understanding or be involved in a community of believers. But Spiritualizers find their worth in these things, not in Christ. That's one reason they are so passionate about causes. If you disagree with their politics or theology, they *have* to prove you wrong because their value as a person is at stake.

This is how they can feed the poor, counsel drug addicts or fight the death penalty and yet have a hateful, self-protective covering over their heart. It's hard to reason with Revolutionary Spiritualizers, because their self-image is intertwined with their cause. If you poke a hole in their cause, you poke a hole in them. If you dare to disagree with them, you will be accused of not valuing truth, Christ—or both.

The tricky thing is that Revolutionary Spiritualizers always have a valid point, but that isn't the issue here. The issue is that these men and women can use their cause as a buffer between them and the rest of the human race. In other words their love for you depends on your degree of concurrence with them. That is not the love of God.

Jesus loved Nicodemus the Pharisee as well as Mary the harlot. He could open his heart to the materialist as well as to the destitute. He wasn't into a cause; he was into people. Revolutionary Spiritualizers are loving too, but only to those on the right side of the fence. Those on the other side are deserving of their contempt or indifference. Once again, that is not the love of God.

What good is it to save babies, support the right candidate or pass out sandwiches to the poor if I have not love? Paul understood this very well. He didn't say that these things shouldn't be done (nor do I); he said that it's not of God if you do these things but refuse to be vulnerable. Every relational mask we've looked at has the same core: a refusal to risk giving and receiving love from certain people. At core it is also a tendency to be selective in what parts of our hearts we allow God to interact with.

> **THINGS SPIRITUALIZERS SAY:**
>
> "Don't worry; it will all work out for the good."
>
> "There's nothing Jesus and I can't handle together."
>
> "He just needs to get right with God."
>
> "If you prayed and read your Bible, you wouldn't have this problem."
>
> "There must be sin in her life."
>
> "How *dare* you imply that I don't love the Lord!"
>
> "I'm not angry."
>
> "The devil is really attacking me today."

The Suffering Spiritualizer. This is the man or woman who suffers in silence. If pressed, they will tell you that they do so because they feel led by God to stay in that situation. They will say they are doing it for the other person's benefit (usually the person hurting them), but this too can be a counterfeit of genuine love: "If I . . . surrender my body to the flames, but have not love, I gain nothing" (1 Corinthians 13:3).

Certainly God calls each of us to a degree of suffering and struggle, but Suffering Spiritualizers misunderstand both suffering and love.

Julia and Thomas served as missionaries to a remote African tribe, but Thomas struggled with pornography. Julia would find it in their compound and see the strange way Thomas acted each time he came back from the city. Once she even found a ticket stub to an adult theater in his pocket.

She knew that her husband was being used by God, but she also knew he had an ever-increasing problem with lust. Julie was an incredible woman of prayer. She prayed for hours that God would speak to Thomas. She fasted. She redoubled her efforts to be more sexually available. For five years she labored silently to love Thomas back to health. When he didn't respond, she prayed and fasted more.

It all came to a head when someone in the tribe accused Thomas of making a sexual advance. When this was brought to the attention of their leaders in the field, Thomas and Julia were sent back to America to deal with their marriage. That's when I got to know them.

Julia is a great example of the Suffering Spiritualizer. She interceded, exercised endless patience and poured as much love on Thomas as she knew how. One thing she didn't do, however, was get honest with him or their leaders about what was going on. The idea of boundaries made little sense to Julia. When I asked her why she didn't confront her husband or speak with their supervisors, she said she was "committing it to God."

I believe she was completely sincere, but she was also hiding behind the mask of "martyrdom." If she had really dealt with the situation, it would have upset her marriage, her ministry and her reputation. That's why she didn't bring anyone else into it (until it became public knowledge). She had to protect her persona of being a spiritual giant serving God on the mission field. For her, being a missionary proved that she was a worthwhile person.

If love is acting in the other person's best interest, regardless of the cost, Julia was not walking in love. To walk in love we must also walk in light (1 John 1:5-7). Julia refused to do that. The most loving thing she could have done for Thomas was say, "Honey, I'm aware of the pornography. I'm insisting that you become accountable to our leaders or I will tell them myself."

Doing that, however, would have upset Julia's world completely.

She was actually protecting her husband's sin and her own security. When she began seeing this, it started making sense to her why God didn't answer her prayers. His Word and his Spirit were telling her to get real about this problem, but she was afraid. She valued her own status quo more than working toward her husband's spiritual growth. She was amazed to see that her spirituality was actually self-centered.

The Suffering Spiritualizer will put up with the most shocking abuse or neglect from spouses, children, bosses and others, but there are times when it isn't loving to myself or others to endure such treatment. The most loving thing is to draw a boundary that says, "It is wrong for you to treat a son or daughter of God this way. I also do you a grave disservice letting you believe this is okay. I am neither living honestly with you nor making you better for other relationships. This mistreatment ends today."

AN AWFUL BIND

My presentation of the types of Spiritualizers may seem one-dimensional. The women and men I've described are much more complex than I have space here to explain. They do truly loving things. They care deeply about evangelism, ministry and missions. They aren't simple Pharisees. (For that matter, the Pharisees weren't simple either.) The Spirit of God is using many of these men and women in awesome ways.

I am not denying these facts. I am only stating another: They are blinded by their gifts and passions to the brokenness that lies deep within their own hearts. They have so much to offer, but in order for them to be *honest* followers of Jesus, they are going to have to face the fear inside. Most Spiritualizers cannot admit fear because that would chip away at the air of perfection that all Spiritualizers maintain.

The Spiritualizer says, "Sure, I have my faults," but he is always general about what those are. Or she will admit only to faults that are socially acceptable, so as not to damage her image. In the end it is their image Spiritualizers trust in—not Jesus Christ. This puts them in an awful bind. They truly want to serve God and others, but doing that well requires a frighteningly honest look inside. Their shame causes them to fear this deeply.

Shame is a deep-seated sense of worthlessness, often too painful even to admit. It is the thing that requires me to look better than I really am. Shame requires that I know the answers or not have any obvious moral flaws. Shame requires that you never suspect I am afraid, lustful, confused or lonely. If I were to come clean about these things, I would have no protection left (except Jesus Christ). Can you see now why Spiritualizers—in spite of their seeming superiority—are living in rank unbelief?

Spiritualizers have formed a relational mask out of their core beliefs. They hold to the "I don't need other people" belief. They think they are complete all by themselves. They hang onto the belief that intimate relationships bring only pain. Yet if they are able to drop their I-have-it-all-together facade, they can be truly immersed in another person. If they do this, they will find that intimacy sometimes brings fulfillment, not the rejection they anticipate.

Spiritualizers hold to a crippling core belief: I must do everything perfectly or I am worthless.

Most important, Spiritualizers hold to a crippling core belief: I must do everything perfectly or I am worthless. This core belief has metastasized into a relational mask that colors their every interaction. These interactions make it impossible for them to love God and others in the way they are capable of doing. But there is hope.

THE SPIRITUALIZER REDEEMED

What do the various Spiritualizers have in common? It isn't doctrine, because you find Spiritualizers in every camp from fundamentalist to liberal. It isn't practice, because you find them in every socio-religious setting. Some are blazing trails in Christian activism, while others distinguish themselves in academia or in power encounters with the supernatural. Temperament isn't the unifying factor either. Some Spiritualizers are very patient and quiet (the Suffering Spiritualizers). Others are bold and authoritative (the Powerful Spiritualizers). Still others are dignified or intellectual (the Insightful or Pedigreed Spiritualizers).

What is the unifying principle then? It is zeal. Every Spiritualizer has a genuine passion to do God's will. The problem is that they misconstrue God's nature, which leads to a misunderstanding of God's will. Spiritualizers often come from homes characterized by abuse, neglect or rigid spirituality. These experiences in childhood shape how they see God as adults. The attitudes and behaviors of Spiritualizers are very consistent with their view of God.

Spiritualizers have a God who is either an *extension* of their dysfunctional parents or a *reaction* to them. For instance, the person raised by passive, nonaffirming parents often grows up to serve one of two Gods. The first God is seen as distant and difficult to read. In order to get acceptance from

---

THINGS SPIRITUALIZERS DO:

- talk a lot
- have a ready answer for every problem
- act uptight, superior or out of touch
- continually rail against certain people, groups or belief systems
- quote the Scriptures often but lack an in-depth understanding
- serve others but often in a condescending way
- major in minors
- fail to see the sin in their lives

him, they must believe and do all the right things. This is the only way the "disinterested God" will take notice and, they hope, offer his acceptance. This is an attempt by Spiritualizers to perpetuate the drama of their family. In so doing they can get the acceptance as an adult that they didn't get as a child.

The second God may be characterized by passion and zeal. This view of God is a reaction to the dysfunctional parenting style this particular Spiritualizer may have been raised with. In effect they envision a God who is everything they wish their parents had been. As a follower of such a God, they seek to emulate him and secretly despise those who are "lukewarm."

Because Spiritualizers are relating to a God who is somewhat distorted, their only hope is to find out who God really is—apart from the extremes on both ends—and zealously follow him. Spiritualizers already have the zeal and a lot of knowledge to go with it. The only problem is that their zeal isn't combined with an *accurate* knowledge (see Romans 10:2-3; 1 Corinthians 8:2; Galatians 4:18).

The challenge for Spiritualizers is to find the true God. Not the God of legalism. Not the God of liberal theology. Not God-as-I-would-like-him-to-be. In 1 Corinthians 13, where we identified the various types of Spiritualizers, we also find a description of love. Paul says in this chapter that genuine love is patient and kind. Genuine love isn't envious, boastful or proud.

Whatever Paul could say about love, he could say about God. His fellow apostle John would agree (see 1 John 4:7-8). If God is love, then the "love chapter" describes him and the characteristics of those who follow him. The God of legalism is a false one because the true God is patient and kind. The true God isn't easily angered and doesn't keep a record of wrongs. The true God always protects, always perseveres and never fails. This is very different from the God of the legalist, the God who is ready to pounce at the slightest hint of failure.

The true God isn't a pushover either. He hates our sexual immorality, dishonesty and selfishness, because all of these destroy the person who engages in them. If God accepted these, he would not be acting in our best interest, and acting in the best interest of the other is love itself.

Paul's description of love mirrors perfectly the description of Jesus we find in the four Gospels. This clear portrayal of God's love continues throughout the rest of the New Testament as well. Yes, God judges (as Scripture also makes clear), but his bias is always in favor of extending mercy to all who will take hold of it.

Spiritualizers operate on the assumption that God needs them to do or be a certain thing before he can accept them. Most Spiritualizers wouldn't say this out loud. In fact, most use the language of grace, but their attitudes and behaviors mirror a life in the shadow of law. So what are Spiritualizers to do? They must become stubborn about finding the true God and aligning themselves with him. They must use their innate passion to seek and find the God who is patient and kind. As they let him invade more and more of their hearts, they will reflect this same patience and kindness. They must zealously seek him to fill all the holes in their self-image. As they do, their boastfulness, pride and rudeness will give way to the gracious manner characteristic of their Savior.

As they continue seeking the true God, they will discover that God has actually been seeking them. This will begin to heal their insecurities and posturing. They will no longer need to be self-seeking, because they have someone far greater and more powerful than themselves seeking their good. They won't be easily angered when others are favored or promoted ahead of them, because they will know that their day in the sun is coming.

Finally, they will be zealous about protecting their own dignity. They will be patient and kind with themselves instead of shaming and condemning. The old self-contempt will give way to a generous spirit that eagerly awaits loving words from the Lord. They will be candid about their sin but not defined by it. They will be defined by their loving Savior and by him alone.

TALE OF A SPIRITUALIZER

One night in our group meeting I was speaking on family-of-origin issues. I was talking about how wounded we can be in the first fifteen years of life without ever acknowledging it as adults. One young man, Andrew, was listening intently. The more I talked, the more his eyes brimmed with tears. Andrew was not afraid to feel his emotions—and he had a lot of them. During a question-and-answer time, he asked about his relationship with his mother.

Andrew's mom was very cold to him as a child, and it left deep wounds and questions about his worth. As he shared his heart, he choked back sobs. Across the room I could see Tom watching Andrew closely. "Tom, did you have something you wanted to share?" I asked.

"Yes, Andrew, as I hear you talking about your pain, it seems to me that you are dwelling on the past." Andrew looked at Tom with a confused expression.

"The Scriptures tell us to 'forget those things that are behind and to press on.'" Tom continued, "God wants us to keep our eyes on Jesus and not look at the waves all around us, even the waves of our past."

Tom followed that with an inspiring story and quoted Luther or Augustine or somebody. I turned to Andrew and asked if Tom's comments were helpful. Andrew responded, almost with a sigh, "Not really."

Tom raised a finger and looked at me, obviously wanting to say more. I wasn't surprised, because Tom always had things to share. Often they were truly edifying. He would quote a Scripture or share an anecdote. He knew church history too and loved to quote great leaders of the past or share one of their experiences.

But Tom made some of us uncomfortable. He wasn't pushy or anything, but he never shared about himself or what he was dealing with. He always taught others, quoted someone or reminded us of a Bible verse. After meeting in our large group, we always broke up into smaller groups. The group I led consisted of six men, and Tom was one of them. I knew it was time for me to say something.

"Tom, you've been in the group now for a few months, and I want you to know that I've appreciated many of the things you've shared, but, Tom, we don't know *you*. We know what you believe and we know that you are knowledgeable, but I have a question for you: Could it be that you use your many words to hide behind?"

As Tom considered my question, about three heads began nodding up and down. "You know, I've never thought of that," he said, "but I think you might be right."

I was so glad that Tom was open and not defensive. "Here's a way I think we could help you," I said. "What if each time you began to 'wax eloquent' [a few chuckled] the group could ask you what is going on in your heart?"

"I'd be open to that," Tom said.

For the rest of that night and each week thereafter, the group did exactly that. When Tom began to talk about "some people" or to say, "Well, Ephesians says . . . " we would stop him. "Let's reel it in, Tom," someone would say. "You're doing it again," someone else would remind him. To his credit, Tom would catch himself and talk about what was going on in his less-than-perfect marriage or about his personal struggles. Tom wasn't quite as "spiritual" after that, but he sure was more honest.

TIPS FOR SPIRITUALIZERS

- Make a practice of telling others about your sins rather than your virtuous life.

- If you impress many people, you probably aren't being honest (see Luke 6:26).
- Learn how to say, "I blew it. I'm so sorry," instead of explaining to others how they added to the problem.
- Assume that your biblical knowledge may not be as complete as you think.
- Focus on doing good rather than looking good.[1]
- Realize (as un-Christian as it might sound) that God isn't enough; you need others.[2]
- Get to know people who are different from you (socially, ethnically and theologically). They may have hidden gifts for you from the Lord.
- The best thing you could do for your children is spend lots of quality time with them (whether you talk about the Lord or not).
- Your spouse needs your affection and practical help, not a sermon.
- Realize that people and institutions will *never* be everything you want them to be.
- Stop trying to impress God with the intensity or sincerity of your repentance.
- The next time you sin, try boldly laying hold of God's grace instead of groveling at his feet (Hebrews 4:16).
- When you are doing good and feeling good, remember that there is still darkness in you (see James 3:2; 1 John 1:8).
- When your sins humiliate you and you feel like a failure, remember: you are still God's priceless, irreplaceable child.

9

THE SECRET TO LIFE WITH GOD

We've talked about everything from Saviors to Spiritualizers, Aggressors to Avoiders. We've seen how the relational masks we wear can cause so much trouble in our relationships. We've looked at concrete ways of dealing with each one. And we've seen how the answer we seek is often hidden within the relational mask itself (if we only know where to find it).

Is there a principle or truth that can be applied to all this? Is there a way of looking at God, ourselves and others that will set us free from our differing relational masks? There is, and I call it *the relational principle*. The relational principle is this: everything God has ever done or will ever do is geared toward the formation of intimate relationships.

> **Everything God has ever done or will ever do is geared toward the formation of intimate relationships.**

God does not want us to be merely good or productive. He wants us to be completely wrapped up in him, and he wants us to enjoy authentic intimacy with each other. These are the only reasons the universe exists. The goal of intimacy is behind everything from creation to the giving of the law. It is behind redemption and the second coming. Intimacy will fill the new heaven and the new earth. Intimacy is God's very heartbeat.

This is why our relational masks are so tragic. If we live life through any of these masks, *we are not being intimate*. No matter how spiritual we may look, if we don't fight against these deep-seated traits in ourselves, we violate the very reason for our existence. In this chapter we will look at the relational principle as it applies to our connection with God. In the next chapter we will see how the relational principle applies to our connection with each other.

THE HEART OF THE UNIVERSE

As Christians, we believe the biblical revelation of God's nature. That revelation tells us that God is triune. Before time began the Father, Son and Holy Spirit enjoyed ceaseless communion with one another. Before anything came to be, there was a joyous dance among the members of the Godhead. God was not bored and he was not lonely.

The Father, the Son and the Holy Spirit were bursting with joy and love. God created us to share in this eternal intimacy. First he set the stage by flinging dazzling stars and planets into an endless space. In the middle of it he put a tiny blue ball. As he continued conducting his orchestra, mountains, forests and animal life sprang into existence. These dizzying wonders appeared as he spoke the powerful word of command.

Then he did something rather strange. He stopped speaking and bent down silently to play in the dirt. He artfully sculpted a masterpiece of clay with his own hands. Then, as if having his hands all over it wasn't enough, he pulled the lifeless hulk close to his face and literally gave him the kiss of life (Genesis 2:7). God didn't have to do it this way. He did it to make a point: as impressive as everything in creation is, this one is different. This man and the woman to come out of him are his absolute pride and joy. Above all things God is into relationship.

Most of us know what happened next. The man and woman stepped out from beneath God's protective covering. When they did this, their ability to be intimate with him and each other died on the spot. This began thousands of years of loneliness, cruelty and frustration.

During the centuries that followed, God gave his law to the Israelites. He also sent them prophets and taught them how to worship. He gave them sacrifices and elaborate rituals to instill in them an appreciation of his holiness. *And all of this was going somewhere.* It was setting us up for intimacy. Even the Old Testament is clear that God never wanted his people to focus on laws or rituals—he wanted relationship:

> "I hate, I despise your religious feasts;
>> I cannot stand your assemblies.
> Even though you bring me burnt offerings and grain offerings,
>> I will not accept them.
> Though you bring choice fellowship offerings,
>> I will have no regard for them.
> Away with the noise of your songs!
>> I will not listen to the music of your harps.
> But let justice roll on like a river,
>> righteousness like a never-failing stream!" (Amos 5:21-24)

The Israelites' sacrifices, feasts and worship services wearied God, even though he had commanded them to observe each one. What he was really after was justice. In other words, he wanted women and men to treat each other with consideration and love. He was also after righteousness, which means relating rightly to God, ourselves and those around us. Righteousness has little to do with external "holiness." God wants us to love one another and to interact honestly with him. This is what Amos is talking about. This is the relational principle.

REMOVING ALL DOUBT

God's revelation to the Israelites was very clear, but most of them missed the relational heartbeat that permeated everything the prophets said. They got lost in a legalistic interpretation of what they thought God wanted.

If there were only a way God could show men and women what he was really like. Some way that he could remove all doubt about his true intentions. This is precisely what God did when he sent Jesus.

Anyone who reads the Gospels can tell you that love characterized everything Jesus ever did. This fact is indisputable. The Scriptures also tell us that looking at the Son is identical to looking at the Father (John 8:19; 12:45; 14:9). When Jesus speaks, it is the Father's voice we hear (John 14:10). Everything Jesus does is exactly what the Father does (John 5:19). If you have any questions about what God is like, Jesus answers them.

Our God on earth was tender to the weak, gracious to the sinful and generous to the needy. He hasn't changed a bit, but his greatest statement, his loudest shout, came from the cross. On the cross our God showed us how deadly serious sin is and what needs to be done to fix it. He also showed you and me how far he is willing to go to have us for himself. As Billy Graham said, "When he stretched out his arms on the cross he was saying, 'I *love* you! I *love* you!'"

Our Lord didn't come to earth simply to conduct mass healing rallies and regional speaking tours. He was hungry to touch, speak to and interact with every person he possibly could. This is why he bent down to play with children. He looked people in the eye and told them wonderful things. He was showing us—if only we can see it—that the eternal heart of God beats for only one purpose: *interaction with us.* This is the relational principle, and it is central to everything God is about.

The answer for everyone under the power of a relational mask is to apply the relational principle to their unique problem. Though the relational principle has universal application, it takes different forms when applied to each of the relational masks. Let's talk nuts and bolts now.

God and the Avoider

As you may have guessed, the number-one problem for the Avoider is avoiding God altogether. But Christians whose avoidant relational masks are still in place won't do this completely. Because they are conscious of God's presence in their lives, there will always be *some* interaction between them. However, this interaction is often rare and inconsistent.

If you are an Avoider, you must learn to risk. Risk may be the one thing you fear most, but it is also your salvation. God will put you in situations where you must act. He will put you in jobs you hate, marriages that are painful and situations that seem unbearable.

It's not that he specially designs these scenarios (life takes care of that by itself), but your avoidant lifestyle will make a tough situation insufferable. Instead of handling problems as they come up, you often let them get worse until things are totally out of control.

It is time for you to take responsibility for your life. Yes, you may have had a painful childhood. You may have been denied the advantages others enjoy. Or you may have health problems or learning disabilities that others don't have to deal with. These don't make it impossible for you to grow—just difficult. The flesh and the devil will lie to you incessantly, saying there is nothing you can do about it. Don't believe it.

The challenge is for you to stay relational. You don't have to love everybody at work but, chances are, God has handpicked some of the problem people there to serve as your teachers. When I was a metal worker I had to work with a man named Pedro. Pedro was rude and demeaning, and I didn't like him at all. One day I was doing something new for me, and I was forced to ask Pedro for help. He began showing me a time-honored trick that he'd learned from twenty years in the business. I thought it sounded goofy and I said so. As he turned to leave he said, "Fine. Do it your way." As you may have guessed, my way didn't work. I was forced to find Pedro and apologize for my ignorance and ask again for his help. God allowed me to be in a situation where I was forced to humble myself. I've been in a lot of those situations.

As an Avoider, you will be tempted to interact with God in ways that are nonrelational. Your bent will constantly pull your prayer or Bible study away from being personal to being mechanical. You may have to learn entirely different ways of getting close to God. You will have to settle it in your mind that connection with God is not optional, any more than eating or sleeping is optional.

When you pray, read, fast or worship, always ask yourself, *Am I being relational?* Don't say the same things in prayer over and over again. Search your heart for the words that come closest to what you are really feeling. Those words may be a little raw or undignified. As an Avoider, it is doubly important for you to risk that kind of honesty.

When you pray, read, fast or worship, always ask yourself, *Am I being relational?*

When you pray, move purposely into areas of past woundedness or anger. Throw off the belief that anger is always bad, and learn to be honest with God about it. The idea of "angry prayer" may sound sacrilegious to you, but you are on firm biblical ground if you express yourself this way to God.[1]

Learn how to bring your body into it. Lift your hands, kneel, sing at the top of your voice. Anything that pulls you out of your safe shell is probably good. Many Avoiders find "theological" reasons why they can't enjoy some of these worship styles. See those as the smokescreens they really are and push through them. You will be amazed at what happens to your heart when you force it to flow out of your body.

Don't read your Bible for the sake of gathering knowledge. When you read, apply to yourself everything that is applicable. This will mean that you have to actually *do* some of the things you are reading about. Find out from leaders you trust if your understanding of a Scripture is accurate and then be ready for God to open a scary door. At that point you have to step through it. Sure, you will make mistakes and look stupid on occasion, but this is the only way you will grow past your fears.

I've had the privilege of seeing Avoiders slowly evolve into powerful disciples of Jesus Christ. I've seen the joy on their faces when they realized they were no longer bound by an old fear. I've seen how families and churches change when avoidant men and women see through the lies they've believed and do the hard thing.

GOD AND THE DEFLECTOR
Of all the relational masks, the Deflector looks the most relational. Deflectors are the ones laughing and talking and connecting. They are the person everybody knows. But as we've demonstrated, Deflectors aren't really relational, they are social—and there's a difference.

God will send people to the Deflector who seem to be negative. In reality they aren't negative but honest. They will push all your buttons if you are a Deflector. It will be easy to write some of these people off because of their bluntness, but God is sending them to you as a wake-up call. The best thing you can learn to do is to share your pain with trustworthy people.

This is hard because, as a Deflector, you may have spent a lifetime wrapping your pain in humor or flamboyance. It's also hard for you to share inner pain because you aren't relating to it yourself. The relational principle holds true for self-awareness too. It's as if the Deflector's heart is a house with many rooms. In the very back is a room that contains all the pain, disappointment and anger in the Deflector's life. For some Deflectors, a court jester stands stationed at the door. Other Deflectors have a spouse, ex-spouse or parent guarding the way. This sentry keeps everyone (including you) from unlocking the secrets of that room.

If you, as a Deflector, become relational with your own true heart, you will find that God is there too. Discipline yourself to cry, rage or feel with a trusted friend as well as with the Lord. It will be hard for you to look at your own reality without cracking a joke or blaming someone else. You have probably been trained in your family to suppress difficult emotions and change the subject. But something you've learned to do can be unlearned with the help of accountability and the Holy Spirit.

One of the best spiritual disciplines for a Deflector is keeping a journal. This is a big challenge for you, but it pays rich dividends. Writing your life story, your feelings or your prayers can clear away much of the deflective fog that keeps you from truth. The other invaluable tool for the Deflector is accountability. If you are a Deflector, you need someone—or a few someones—who will call you on the carpet when you are too funny, blaming or conversational. It will feel as if they are cramping your style, but in reality they are bringing you back to center.

The ultimate deflection is to blame your problems on God. Adam showed us how this worked when God asked if he'd eaten from the tree. He said, "The woman *you put here* with me—she gave me some fruit from the tree, and I ate it" (Genesis 3:12, emphasis added). See,

Lord, I was minding my own business when you gave me this temptress and everything went to pot! As a Deflector, when you come to God in prayer, learn how to zero in on *your* stuff.

The Bible can easily become a dead book for you as well. The reason for this is you will often read something and realize that it describes someone you know. You will be filled with a passion to share this insight with that individual, never realizing that it was intended for you. You may find that you have keen insight into the failings of others but fail to see your own weaknesses. If you will let the Scriptures judge you instead of applying them to everyone else, you will be amazed at how personal and relevant the Bible becomes.

If you learn how to listen to criticism that is truly constructive, read the Bible for yourself and keep yourself honest as you pray, freedom will come. You won't have to lighten the mood with a joke or turn the spotlight on another person's sins. True peace and joy always come out of that part of us that is closest to the core. If you will courageously embrace the pain behind the smile, your true joy will eventually emerge. Scripture attests to this.

> Even in laughter the heart may ache,
> and joy may end in grief. (Proverbs 14:13)

> Those who sow in tears
> will reap with songs of joy.
> He who goes out weeping,
> carrying seed to sow,
> will return with songs of joy,
> carrying sheaves with him. (Psalm 126:5-6)

GOD AND THE SELF-BLAMER

You would think Self-Blamers could find their way to God the most quickly. In spite of how it appears, Self-Blamers are not experts at repentance. Far from it. They are experts at self-focus, but the focus is totally negative and dark. This is not repentance; it's obsession.

For Self-Blamers to be relational with God, they must turn against the negative self-focus. This will be hard because they have learned over the years to "get high" on this feeling. As with the person who is constantly angry, chemicals are released in the brain that cause a type of euphoria. As weird as it sounds, Self-Blamers feel good when they feel bad.

**Self-Blamers are experts at self-focus,
but the focus is totally negative and dark.
This is not repentance; it's obsession.**

Letting go of this lifelong addiction will be very tough. It's the only real identity the Self-Blamer has ever had. That's why it's crucial for him to lay hold of the grace of God. If this is your particular relational mask, let me say to you again: You must wrap yourself around God's grace and never let go.

Even this can become a trap if you say, "See, I can't even do *that!*" But that's the wondrous thing about God's grace: he gives it even to those who are really bad at receiving it. You must learn everything you can about this subject. Read every book, listen to every tape and watch every video you can get your hands on. Of course books and videos aren't enough. What you need most is a gracious man or woman of God to get close to.

Dare to believe that this man or woman sees you more clearly than you see yourself. You have good reason to question your judgment anyway. So listen to the servant of God who teaches you about grace and demonstrates it for you.

When you talk to God, do it in the name of Jesus. I don't mean tack "in Jesus' name" at the end of every prayer. I mean come to God in the grace, power and sinlessness that Jesus' name embodies. Each time you come to God with that mindset, you are saying, "Here I am again, Lord. I know you will hear me and love me and care for me because I come through the gateway of your perfect, all-powerful Son."

> **That's the wondrous thing about God's grace:**
> **he gives it even to those who are really**
> **bad at receiving it.**

I was at church one Sunday morning preparing to worship. As I looked around, I saw several beautiful women. My heart responded with a lustful hunger. Just then the music began and the people around me started singing. I felt filthy and hopeless. *I can't even worship God because I'm such a pervert!* I considered leaving, but then a picture flashed into my mind. I saw myself standing alone on a stone pavement with my hands lifted heavenward. The pavement was literally covered with blood. I knew immediately what God was trying to show me: I don't worship him based on my pure heart; I come to him upheld by the very blood of his Son.

Learn to see the many gifts that God gives you. Do you have a family? A car? A job? Are you in good health? Every one of these gifts has a card attached to it that reads, "I love you completely. Signed, God." This is the definitive statement about your worth. Trust no other voice! Not even your own. You must hold on to whatever word pictures or symbols God gives you that speak of his grace.

Read Romans, Galatians, Ephesians and Colossians, but don't tell yourself they are written for somebody else. They are written for you. They are written for people who need mercy and grace. Root the truth of these books deep into your soul. Remember, your heart can sometimes be a hateful bully (1 John 3:20), and it will wallop you every chance it gets. When that happens, fall into the arms of love and lie still.

For you, the relational principle means that you choose to continually look at Jesus. You choose to relate to him, not to your sin or self-hate. Find out who God really is. Peel off the religious veneer that covers his loving heart. See him touch the leper, the prostitute and the rip-off artist (Mark 1:40-42; Luke 7:36-50; 19:1-10). Realize that he touches you with that same grace.

Sometimes you will feel God's love; sometimes you won't. Don't let your heart fool you. He is a person, not a feeling. As you continue to take your stand on his grace, in time your emotions will follow suit. Peter was a man acquainted with self-hate, but he walked with Jesus for many years. What were some of the final words of this old man? What did he want us to remember? "This is the true grace of God. Stand fast in it" (1 Peter 5:12).

GOD AND THE SAVIOR

Do you see traits of the Savior in your life? Do you spend most of your time preoccupied with another person's needs? Are you good at giving but really bad at receiving? If these describe you, take heart; there is hope! Just as Jesus came to liberate Martha from her self-imposed work ethic, he comes to liberate you.

Saviors are already skilled at helping others (albeit with a dysfunctional motive). The skill they lack is the ability to be *ministered to*. If you want to be truly relational with God, you must let him touch you in areas that make you uncomfortable. For Saviors, the relational principle is active when he can rest and receive from Jesus. As funny as it might sound, rest is a sacrament, and the Savior who wants to be whole must observe this sacrament.

When you are tempted to feel useless because you're not doing anything for anybody, discipline yourself to be still in God's love for you. Sandra, a Savior I'd been counseling for a while, had a really hard time with this. I pleaded with her to slow down, but that didn't make any sense to her. I knew she found her worth in helping and doing for others. Then she got really sick.

In the hospital, she was forced to stay in bed and let people wait on her. She hated it! When family or friends came to visit, she felt so ashamed. She was ashamed because she wasn't *doing* anything. Of course she got out of bed before she was supposed to, and of course she insisted on going home before she was well.

But finally God began to break through. What did Sandra do? She disciplined herself to be still and let God love her. She learned to pray, "Lord, what would you like to tell me today?" Sometimes he spoke of himself and sometimes he spoke to her about her. She learned how to receive God's affirmation of *who she was,* not just what she did.

Like Sandra, we Saviors have to let *the* Savior save us. When you talk to him, be bold enough to ask him to touch you. To speak to you. To encourage you. And to spoil you. This feels all wrong at first, but you will get used to it. In fact, if you listen carefully to what Jesus whispers to your mind, you will be amazed at how complimentary he can be.

You may have been taught not to be selfish. Rightly understood that's a good thing, but if you search God's Word carefully, you will find many godly people praying for themselves. In fact, it's overwhelming. The greatest example of this is Psalms. A hundred and fifty chapters of hear me, answer me, save me, love me. I'm exaggerating a little bit, but you get the idea.

The greatest servant of all asked his Father and others to meet his needs (see Matthew 26:37-39; 27:46; Luke 5:2-3; John 4:7; 17:5). On one occasion Jesus took a nap while his disciples did the work (Mark 4:35-38). You too must learn to take care of your body and nourish your soul. This isn't selfish; it's sensible.

The greatest servant of all asked his Father and others to meet his needs.

The relational principle doesn't apply only to you and God or you and others. It also applies to you being rightly related to yourself. Are you abusing your body and mind through overeating, sleep deprivation or constant stress? Running yourself into the ground doesn't glorify God. Yes, there will be times of hard work for every servant, but the master also wants you to rest. Jesus said, "Come with me by yourselves to a quiet place and get some rest" (Mark 6:31).

The greatest rest of all is resting in the loving arms of Jesus (Matthew 11:28-30). This must become a key prayer focus for you. Yes, pray for others in public and in private, but learn to lift up your needs and desires as well—without shame. Humble yourself enough to ask your brothers and sisters to lay hands on you and pray for your needs (James 5:14-16).

Step down from your pedestal and allow God and others to touch you. Believe that God wants to do wonderful things for you. Many times God's blessing on your life enriches others, but sometimes God's blessing is a personal gift only for you. Don't leave hundreds of gifts unclaimed beneath the tree. Open them and enjoy them. When you do this, it always splashes onto those around you.

GOD AND THE AGGRESSOR

We've all heard of criminals who were intelligent and industrious. How many times have we said, "If he put that same energy into making an honest living, he'd be a millionaire"? It is similar for Aggressors. They have boundless energy and drive, but they often apply it in the wrong direction. The easiest thing in the world for the Aggressor to do is run himself ragged with Christian activities or ministry. At the end of his life, however, it will become a hollow victory if he hasn't learned the relational principle.

For Aggressors, working for God is often done in an intimacy vacuum. Even "quiet time" is often prep time for some ministry activity. The brawny construction worker can operate a jackhammer but not necessarily play the violin. The reason is that these two activities require different muscles and sensitivities. Similarly, you as an Aggressor may be overdeveloped in ministry but underdeveloped in intimacy.

The answer for you is to take that same drive, that same power, and direct it toward the private world of interacting with God. Like those with the Savior relational mask, you must learn to spend time with God for your own sake. Certainly you can pray for others, intercede for missionaries or lift your ministry up to God, but you also need to grow a private world of prayer where you come to God only to love him and be loved by him. I cannot emphasize this enough. You will know you're doing it right if you feel completely selfish in your interaction with God. Don't worry, this will pass. In time your private life with Jesus will become so rich that you naturally begin incorporating others.

Every Christian leader I've ever counseled struggled with this problem. That's why everyone is so surprised when Pastor So-and-so runs off with the church secretary. He may have been a brilliant biblical expositor, but he didn't know how to get the deep needs of his heart met by God.

Some of these same leaders have told me, "I spend time with God every day," but when I ask them how Jesus has loved them personally—outside a ministry context—they often don't have an answer. The best thing you could do for yourself or those you serve is to become proficient at being vulnerable with your heavenly friend.

God doesn't want you merely to fill a position in the great enterprise of heaven. He wants to fill *you* up. He didn't say, "I have come that you may work your tail off and do it more abundantly." He said that he came to give you fullness of life (John 10:10). The Bible's emphasis is not on ministry, bearing fruit or being a soul winner. It is on relationship: if you *follow* him, he will make you a fisher of people (Mark 1:17). If you *abide* in him, you will "bear much fruit" (John 15:5). If you *live* by the Spirit, you will not "gratify the desires of the sinful nature" (Galatians 5:16).

The American body of Christ is geared toward programs and numbers. We are the most prayerless and biblically illiterate Christians in the world. On the whole we do not truly believe in the relational principle. Yet if we pursued this passionately, ministry would flow out of us all by itself. If you fall into the nonrelational trap, I implore you to seek Jesus with no agenda other than letting him love you.

The Bible's emphasis is not on ministry, bearing fruit or being a soul winner. It is on relationship.

Table 9.1 draws a contrast between what we often do as Christians and what is more intimate. The items designated *nonrelational* are not necessarily bad. Neither are they inappropriate for the new believer as she develops into a more relational person. Many of these practices are good, but they often fail to bring us into the immediate presence of God. If the relational principle is accurate, this distinction is an important one to make.

Come to him like David, crying out for him to touch you. Learn to talk with God about your marriage, your parenting and your loneliness. Tell him you need to hear his words of love spoken to your heart. Develop the sensitive muscles of your spiritual ears. Don't be like the ones Jesus turns away in Matthew 7:22-23 who do all kinds of ministry stuff but are never relational with him. Even if we assume that he is talking about people who aren't truly saved, the point is still clear: *He wants us to be relational.* Everything else is secondary.

Our Lord told the spiritual leaders of his day that they did not know the Scriptures (Matthew 22:29). Yet they were the Scripture experts! He also said they knew nothing about the power of God. And what is the power of God? Is it signs and wonders? Impressive evangelistic outreaches? No, the power of God is love. The Christian who is relational with God and lets him search out every corner of her heart is the person with real power. The person who has this power with God will have power with people.

When you pray, do it in such a way that the clothes come off your soul. Don't avoid this type of transparency by surrounding yourself with busyness. When you study the Scriptures, they should not be an end in themselves. You can be aggressive about reading or memorizing and still not read the Scriptures in a relational way: "You diligently study the Scriptures because you think that by them you possess eternal life. These are the Scriptures that testify about me, yet you refuse to come to me to have life" (John 5:39-40).

In all our praying, reading and worshiping we must come to Jesus. Don't assume that because you read the Bible or use the right God-talk you are being relational. The woman who is practicing the relational principle will read God's Word knowing that Jesus' very voice is before her eyes and in her heart. And she will listen carefully. The man who is practicing the relational principle will pray in a way that makes him uncomfortable due to its level of vul-

Table 9.1. Interacting with God

	Nonrelational	Relational
Prayer	Saying the words or phrases you think God wants to hear	Saying to God what is actually in your heart (Psalm 51:6)
	Quoting God's Word to him because he is obligated to act on it	Quoting God's Word because it expresses what you are feeling
	Praying loudly, passionately or in a certain manner because you think it gets God's attention	Offering prayer (both verbal and nonverbal) with a quiet confidence that he always hears you (Psalms 19:14; 28:6; 34:15)
	Kneeling, standing or lifting your hands because you think it is expected of you	Kneeling, standing or lifting your hands because it matches the tone of your heart (Lamentations 3:41)
	Saying "in Jesus' name" at the end of every prayer to make it "official"	Praying with a full knowledge that you are totally accepted by the Father because of Jesus
Bible Study	Reading through the Bible in a year so you can say that you did it	Taking whatever time you need to understand and experience Jesus
	Focusing on definitions, histories or word studies so you can be knowledgeable	Focusing on experiencing the presence of God regardless of the Bible study method
	Memorizing Scripture in the belief that having it in your mind changes you	Understanding Scripture and applying it in relationships (James 1:22; 1 John 2:5; 3:18)
	Focusing on the right translation so you know you have God's true Word	Understanding the heart of God in Scripture and interacting with him (regardless of translation)
	Studying to answer skeptics and cultists or to win arguments	Studying to know God better and become an authentic worshiper

Table 9.1. Interacting with God (continued)

	Nonrelational	Relational
Fasting	Going without food so God will know you are serious	Going without food to clear mind and body for deeper intimacy with Jesus
	Going without food because "spiritual" people are expected to fast	Going without food when your heart or the Spirit indicates that it will aid your intimacy with Jesus
	Going without food to show your flesh who is boss	Going without food so you can forget about yourself and feast on Jesus
Spiritual Warfare	Yelling at demons and ordering them around	Fighting to bring your heart in line with God's heart
	Focusing on what Satan is doing in various locations	Focusing on *God* and what he is doing in various locations
	Looking for the demonic in every sinful behavior	Interacting honestly with God and yourself to uncover the motives behind your sin (Psalms 4:4; 19:12; Lamentations 3:40)
	Assuming there is a demonic source behind every painful or difficult experience	Knowing that pain or difficulty might be the instrument God is using to make you dependent on him (Psalm 119:67; 2 Corinthians 12:7-9)
Worship	Singing certain songs or praising and worshiping a certain way because it feels good	Singing, dancing or praising because it is an accurate reflection of your heart at that moment
	Using a certain form or style of music in worship because it is the only "true" way to worship God	Using a certain form or style of music because it honestly expresses *your heart* to God (John 4:23)

nerability. He will touch hearts with the most passionate lover in the universe.

What I'm describing is not a feeling or emotion. Two people can be deeply intimate without feeling overwhelming emotions, and two strangers can have an intense sexual experience without knowing anything about each other. Intimacy is purposely exposing the embarrassing parts of your life to Jesus and learning, over time, that he will not shame you. Intimacy is a willingness to be totally exposed as a fraud by God's Word, yet know that you are safe in his love.

To the Aggressors in Isaiah's day God said this:

"In repentance and rest is your salvation,
      in quietness and trust is your strength,
      but you would have none of it.
You said, 'No, we will flee on horses.'
      Therefore you will flee!
You said, 'We will ride off on swift horses.'
      Therefore your pursuers will be swift!
A thousand will flee
      at the threat of one;
at the threat of five
      you will all flee away,
till you are left
      like a flagstaff on a mountaintop,
      like a banner on a hill."

Yet the LORD longs to be gracious to you;
      he rises to show you compassion.
For the LORD is a God of justice.
      Blessed are all who wait for him! (Isaiah 30:15-18)

Put down your five-year plans and all the projects you believe will validate your existence and come to him, who alone can shower you with the love and compassion you need. Blessed are all who wait for him.

GOD AND THE SPIRITUALIZER

Spiritualizers are truly a mixed bag. On the one hand, their knowledge of Scripture and commitment to prayer is sincere, and they really do care about the people they minister to. On the other hand, Spiritualizers carry deep fears, which they cover up with their "spirituality." Of course we should all bring our fears to Jesus and let him wrap them in his presence, but that's not what Spiritualizers do. They hide behind Christianity and do not—or cannot—deal with the insecurities that subconsciously threaten them.

Every Spiritualizer attempts to solve their problems according to their understanding of God. Powerful Spiritualizers will seek out prayer or attend a meeting where they can be instantly delivered from their defects of character. Insightful Spiritualizers will search for new information that will answer their questions and change their life. Pedigreed Spiritualizers will turn to ancient texts, symbols or rituals to obtain the change they seek. Revolutionary Spiritualizers will redouble their efforts at working on the cause. They believe that if they attack the social issues they feel so strongly about, they will be transformed along the way. Suffering Spiritualizers believe they will change if they can enter into their sufferings more completely.

All Spiritualizers insist on ordering their life according to their theology, philosophy or unique understanding of sanctification. The problem is, it allows the superspiritual relational mask to stay intact. What Spiritualizers really need is to allow Jesus to lead them into the difficult experiences of life that will show them who they really are.

The places that Jesus will take Spiritualizers causes a terrible shock to their system: Powerful Spiritualizers face a trial in their life that no amount of faith seems to change. Insightful Spiritualizers find themselves dealing with a problem that none of their knowledge seems to address. Pedigreed Spiritualizers experience some calamity that doesn't care if they are Catholic or Protestant. Revolutionary Spiritualizers are taken to the place where they see the hypocrisy in their own heart and realize they are just like their enemies. And Suffering Spiritualizers experience increasingly greater pain until they understand that no amount of self-mortification will solve their problem.

When (or if) you finally step into this valley, you will lose all confidence in yourself, your understanding and your assumed superiority. At this point you may even question Christianity itself. This is an awful experience for anyone who goes through it, but it is the only way something as stubborn as a relational mask can be torn off.

Why does God do this? Usually it isn't him doing it. Rather, it's the limitations of the Spiritualizer's approach to life finally bottoming out. Of course Jesus has been telling him for years to expect exactly this kind of trial. The Spiritualizer has agreed in principle that it is required in order to grow, but stepping into the loss or pain in actual experience is always more frightening and jarring than he ever expected.

What the Spiritualizer does with this "dark night of the soul" will determine whether her relational mask hardens around her or buckles and falls away. The Spiritualizer has a choice in this matter; she doesn't have to go the way of genuine honesty. When the crisis hits, she can circle the wagons and protect her way of doing things or abandon the wagons and let Jesus lead her somewhere she's never gone. If she chooses the latter, she will find the Holy Spirit dismantling her personality as she knows it and making her into something different.

This is the very change Spiritualizers fear most. In a sense they are keeping God at bay with their theology, hard work or fixed attitude. If these things were to crumble, they wouldn't know who they were anymore. Many Spiritualizers will fight to the death before they let that happen.

If you are a Spiritualizer, what can you do? Simply this: Let Jesus take you where he wants you to go. And where he takes you will always be a place where your dreams seem to die. Your church may fold. Your health may fail. Your holiness may collapse in a frightening avalanche of sin. Your perfectly ordered world may not stay that way.

If you allow God to lead you through this personal crisis (and if you choose not to fall back on your familiar coping mechanisms), there will certainly be a death of sorts. This death will feel very real to you, but without this death—and your voluntary submission to it—there can be no resurrection.

Each time you step up to this door, you have a fresh opportunity either to go in or to begin another years-long cycle back to this spot. My own crisis came in two parts. The first was when my marriage began unraveling. As a pastor, I was ashamed to go to a counselor and look at issues. I believed such counseling was of the devil. God surprised me by meeting me there and helping me face an abusive and terrifying childhood that I'd tried to ignore. This ancient pain caused me to be emotionally and sexually dependent on my wife in a way that was very unhealthy.

The second part of the crisis came two years later. I thought my wife and I were doing fine and figured the old pain was a thing of the past. On one particular day, we clashed over the same issue. This time I didn't deal with it at an intellectual level; I felt the emotions of it. I felt a loneliness and abandonment that I hadn't tasted since I was fourteen.

I took a long walk and cried out to Jesus to save me. He didn't. At least not in the way I wanted him to. He allowed me to feel the emotions I'd suppressed since childhood. He didn't make the bad feelings or situation go away. What he did was violently tear my hands off the thing I was holding on to. It was the most exquisite pain I've ever felt, but I haven't been the same since.

I'm aware that there may be another door behind that one, but I am confident that Jesus will take me through it, because he was able to keep me alive through the first one. Have all of my spiritualizing tendencies died out? No, but now I see them coming sooner and I am able to let my shame be public without feeling the need to hide it. The thing I once feared most is becoming my source of greatest power.

If you haven't gone to this place I've been talking about, don't try to put yourself there. God will bring it around the moment you have the ego strength to bear it. What you can do until that day is learn to pray as honestly as you can. Confront your theology of God. Is your God tame and predictable, or does your theology allow for God to mess up your life in all the right ways? Will you become hopelessly angry with God because he hasn't behaved the way you wanted him to, or will you follow him into the darkness if he commands it?

There is one more thing Spiritualizers can do if they want to be cooperative with God's working in their life: they can make themselves truly vulnerable to at least two or three people. As Jesus brings people to you who are trustworthy, try to share with them those parts of yourself that are totally humiliating. If you don't know what those are, ask your good friend to tell you what she sees. Find out what brokenness is, at least in theory, so that when you get there you won't lose hope.

WHAT'S UP HIS SLEEVE

This process of being broken applies to each of the relational masks we've discussed. The Avoiders, the Spiritualizers and all the rest must pass through this furnace if they want to be whole. Upon arriving at the furnace, we will question everything we know about God and wonder if he is really good after all. This is perfectly normal. For example, at first Job acknowledged that God created him, but only to crush him. He claimed that everything God did was secretly moving toward a sinister purpose:

Your hands shaped me and made me.
>Will you now turn and destroy me?
Remember that you molded me like clay.
>Will you now turn me to dust again?
Did you not pour me out like milk
>and curdle me like cheese,
clothe me with skin and flesh
>and knit me together with bones and sinews?
You gave me life and showed me kindness,
>and in your providence watched over my spirit.

But this is what you concealed in your heart,
>and I know that this was in your mind. (Job 10:8-13)

When we go through the death Jesus promised, we often feel like Job. But God did not create us to destroy us. He is not a sadist fattening us for the kill. His real agenda is to work in our lives and bring us to fullness of joy (John 15:11). But standing between us and our joy are the sins, core beliefs and relational masks in our hearts. For us to step into that joy, God must clear out the debris that blocks his way.

God takes no pleasure in our suffering, but he sees the situation better than we do, and he is working overtime to bring us to the place where we secretly long to be. As you take your mind off the devil, the boss or the spouse, you will see that *you* are the greatest enemy of your own good. Jesus will give you the desires of your heart, but you must travel the relational road. Everything you carry on the journey that is nonrelational will eventually be stripped off, but in the end, no woman or man who lets Jesus have his way will regret it.

10

THE SECRET TO
LIFE WITH OTHERS

Throughout this book we've seen how those bound behind relational masks dodge authentic relating. In the last chapter we saw how the relational principle can free us from this trap, enabling us to genuinely connect with God. Now let's see how the relational principle is applied to our everyday relationship with ourselves (see table 10.1) and others.

The two great commandments tell us to be relational with God and our neighbor. For the vast majority of us, our nearest neighbor is our spouse. If we aren't practicing the relational principle with our spouse, our Christianity will never leave the starting blocks. Yet this is often where we struggle the most.

In his outstanding book *The Five Love Languages,* Gary Chapman says that each person communicates in a unique "language." Each of us yearns primarily for one or two of these five things: gifts, acts of service, words of affirmation, physical touch or quality time. If a husband's primary love language is acts of service, his wife is not loving him in a way that meets his needs if she compliments him every day (words of affirmation) or puts love notes in his lunch (gifts). The husband whose love language is acts of service feels loved when his wife prepares a meal or maintains the house.

Similarly, if a wife craves quality time with her husband and all he does is buy her lots of stuff, she will not feel loved. Flowers, helping around the house or sexual touch won't mean much if what she longs for is leisurely walks around the block or honest conversation over coffee.

To complicate matters, God almost never puts two people together who speak the same language. You cannot speak *your* language to your spouse; you must find out what *hers* is and become proficient at that. This will take time, patience and a commitment to God to love the other person. However, when two people discover what the other deeply wants and seek to give it, beautiful music begins to play.

My primary love languages are words of affirmation and physical touch. Naturally, these are what I give to others, including my wife. But her languages are acts of service and gifts. As you can imagine, most of my praise, compliments and sexual advances basically fall on deaf ears. My wife doesn't necessarily yearn for those—I do.

This created lots of frustration and heartache for us until we grasped the love languages concept. Now I try to straighten up around the house or bring home the groceries that she needs. This makes her feel very loved. Occasionally I'll put a rose on the dinner table or take her out to eat. These gifts and practical acts are the key to my wife's heart. This is what it looks like for me to love her (see Ephesians 5:25). This is what it looks like for me to be considerate and respectful (see 1 Peter 3:7).

My wife is learning to speak my love languages as well. Though she enjoys sex, it's not at the top of her list. But she is learning to make it a priority because she loves me and wants to speak my dialect. She's also not big on compliments. Her need for words of affirmation is negligible, and she doesn't place the same importance on them that I do. Yet because she loves me, she is learning to thank me and affirm me when I do the little things she appreciates.

Being sexual or affirming is how Keri submits to me and my unique love needs (see Ephesians 5:22-24; 1 Peter 3:1-6). She is never more ravishing to me than when the unfading beauty of her inner self is ex-

Table 10.1. Interacting with Self

	Nonrelational	Relational
Spiritually	Neglecting prayer, Bible study or worship because it feels like a "duty"	Embracing prayer, Bible study and worship because you see it as indispensable for the maintenance of your soul and spirit (Proverbs 19:8)
	Indulging in sin—great or small—because it gives you pleasure and because you think you can't help it	Doing everything in your power to *overcome* sin because you know that sin is the undoing of your very life (Proverbs 1:32; 6:32)
	Obeying God and submitting to his discipline because you think you're supposed to	Obeying God and submitting to his discipline because you know it will eventually lead to joy (Proverbs 4:20-22; John 8:31-32; Hebrews 12:10-11)
Mentally	Reading, thinking or assimilating any information that is enjoyable, regardless of its long-term effects on your mind	Rejecting what is harmful to your mind (regardless of how pleasurable) and pursuing thoughts that are enriching (Psalm 101:3; Philippians 4:8)
	Being content with shallow, clichéd thought processes because they are easier	Applying your mind vigorously and replacing your prejudices with truth—no matter how challenging (Proverbs 3:13-15; 1 Corinthians 3:18; 8:2)
Emotionally	Keeping things bottled up so you don't disturb your comfortable life	Exploring and expressing deep emotions and giving yourself permission to feel them appropriately (Ecclesiastes 3:1, 4; 7:3-4; Matthew 5:4; Mark 14:33; Romans 12:15; Ephesians 4:26; Philippians 4:4; James 4:9)

Table 10.1 Interacting with Self (continued)

	Nonrelational	Relational
Physically	Seeing your body as an impediment to spiritual growth	Seeing your body as crucial to spiritual growth and respecting the mind/body connection (Romans 6:13; 1 Corinthians 6:18-20; 2 Corinthians 4:10; Philippians 1:20)
	Neglecting or abusing your body through overeating, lack of exercise or not seeking medical care	Being sensitive to what your body needs (food, rest, exercise and so on) and maintaining a vital connection to it (Ephesians 5:29)
	Seeing your body in a hateful way because you are "old," "skinny" or "fat"	Cherishing your body in spite of its flaws because God is its architect (Psalm 139:13-16)
Sexually	Being ashamed of your sexuality and feeling uncomfortable with married sex	Enjoying the earthly, sensual pleasures of sex with your spouse (Proverbs 5:15-20; Song of Songs 1—8)
	Abusing your sexuality through affairs, pornography or inappropriate fantasy	Keeping the sexual part of you engaged in a healthy way by abstinence (if you're single) or faithfulness (if you're married). Resisting any thoughts or practices that pull you away from honest sexuality in marriage (1 Corinthians 7:3-5; 1 Thessalonians 4:3-8)
Socially	Believing that you are not worthy to interact with other people	Believing that you are entitled to respect and carrying yourself accordingly (1 Timothy 4:12)
	Constantly doing or saying things to prove to others that you are special, gifted or attractive	Being content either to shine or take a back seat, depending on what God or the situation directs you to do (Philippians 4:11-13)

pressed in terms I can understand. It may be totally different for you and your spouse. Your spouse may put different languages at the top of his or her list, but if you want to practice the relational principle, you must learn how to satisfy your mate's special kind of need.

WHAT ABOUT BOUNDARIES?

What if you've given your spouse what she wants and she still isn't satisfied? Are you supposed to try harder? No. Remember the premise of the relational principle: always give to the other what is *good* for her. If I am a sexual addict, it would no longer be good for my wife to say yes to my every sexual wish. It would be like giving gallons of ice cream to someone with an eating disorder.

Similarly, if your spouse's primary language is gifts, that doesn't mean you allow him to max out the credit card. That would not be loving on your part but, rather, enabling. Our brokenness and our love languages usually occupy the same space in our hearts. The legitimate side of your spouse's love language must be respected and acted upon, but the broken, all-consuming side of it must not be indulged.

No man or woman can ever fill another person's tank to capacity. That type of bottomless need requires a bottomless resource, and if we try to fill that part of another person's soul, we are taking God's job. That can never be good or loving. The relational principle won't steer us wrong here. It will always direct us to give just what is needed but never more than God intends.

BIG SOULS, LITTLE BODIES

How about our children? Is our job as parents simply to shuttle them from soccer and ballet and to keep them stocked up with the latest techno-gadgets? Or has God called us to something more basic than that? In this relationship, as with every other, we are called to be relational.

Deuteronomy tells us how to teach our children God's commands:

"Talk about them when you sit at home and when you walk along the road, when you lie down and when you get up" (6:7). God isn't just telling us to pound Scripture into their heads. He's telling us to interact with them all the time—day and night, driving in the car and getting into bed. You can send your children to every Sunday school and youth group in the world, but if you don't talk, play and move into their space, you are not being relational.

The key isn't teaching; it's relating. If I'm interested when my son talks with me about Spider-Man or Wolverine, then he will be interested when I talk with him about the kingdom of God. If I play cards or Barbies with my daughter, she will want to interact with me about Jesus Christ. Satan tempts us as parents to be so busy that we miss the golden relational opportunities that are right in front of us.

Some of the best conversations I've had with my kids were in the car. In the time it takes for my son and me to drive to the skate shop, we've discussed everything from creationism to eschatology. When my daughter and I go to the store, we discuss God, dating and everything in between.

My friend Randy was fixing up his house so he could put it on the market. During this time he was running around like a crazy man, making repairs and getting everything ready. One day, as he hurried through the living room, he passed by his three-year-old sitting in front of a pile of blocks. The little boy said with a commanding voice, "Daddy, sit down and *play* with me!"

Randy had started to say something about "Daddy being busy" when he felt the Holy Spirit stop him in his tracks. The image of an old man regretting missed opportunities flashed through his mind. In that moment he knew that the most important thing in all the universe was for him to play on the floor with his son. As Randy told me this story, he began to cry. "Russell," he said, "I was forgetting that relationships are eternal. Nothing else matters."

Yes, we have chores to do, checkbooks to balance and dinners to make. But in all of time and eternity, what really matters most? Relationships. Nobody, at life's end, will ever say, "I wish I'd spent more time at the office." Above your children's grades, above giving them everything they want and above giving them the "best opportunities," they need one thing supremely: they need you.

Our sinful nature works in concert with our culture to make many of us so busy that we miss the good stuff. The Holy Spirit has to show us how to love and delight in our children. Even if our own parents didn't do this for us, we can still learn. If you are relational with Jesus on a moment-to-moment basis, he will show you how to be relational with these priceless souls.

**Nobody, at life's end, will ever say,
"I wish I'd spent more time at the office."**

FOCUS ON THE FAMILY OF GOD

Paul tells us, "Be devoted to one another in brotherly love. Honor one another above yourselves" (Romans 12:10). The New Testament is full of commands like this. As far as God is concerned, he wants those of us in the body of Christ to be relational (see table 10.2). We all know this but aren't really good at practicing it.

Sitting next to each other at church on Sunday morning is not relational. Many of the things that pass for "fellowship" are not relational. God wants us to get into one another's lives, but we'll have to push past much of our Christian subculture to do it.

Small groups are not just another fad in the church; they are essential to it. Only in small groups can we really get to know one another. These can be official groups focused on recovery, Bible study or fellowship. Or they can be groups that meet for dinner or simply to "hang out." If you aren't sharing your *inmost* heart with at least a few believers, you are not in God's will, because God's will hinges on the relational principle.

I belong to a very weird little church. We don't have a choir or state-of-the-art Sunday school. My pastor once served with a church that excelled in these things, but it almost killed him. He determined to form a family and teach that family how to be relational. When we do a men's retreat, we don't have five hours of preaching, special music and a host of fascinating activities to choose from. We eat, we talk, and we tell stories.

For three days.

That's it.

Sure, worship and study usually happen at some point, but the agenda is not to do a "Christian thing"; the agenda is to talk, laugh and come to love each other more deeply. I have left each of these retreats feeling so full I could barely stand it. I've been to Promise Keepers events, Christian conferences and every type of religious setting you can imagine. These have all been good, but they are not what the church is for.

The church is for relationships— deep relationships.

The church is for relationships—deep relationships: "Above all, love each other deeply, because love covers over a multitude of sins" (1 Peter 4:8). The typical Sunday-morning service is fine, but if that's all you've got, you've got next to nothing. We want relationships that become intimate in a short time. Yet that's not how the human heart works. It often takes decades for people to become intimate. This is

Table 10.2. Interacting with Others

	Nonrelational	Relational
Spouse	Overfocusing on working, paying the bills, taking care of the house and so on	Making sure you have face-to-face time with your spouse and not using busyness as a substitute (Psalm 127:2; Ecclesiastes 9:9; Colossians 3:19)
	Focusing on helping your spouse lose weight, change bad habits or take responsibility	Focusing on talking, spending time together and being sexually intimate
	Using anger, silence or obvious displeasure to communicate your feelings	Telling your spouse *directly* what you feel and think, without manipulative games (Matthew 5:37; Ephesians 4:25)
	Focusing on children, meetings or private leisure activities	Focusing on developing and nurturing friendship with your spouse as a top priority (Ephesians 5:28-31)
Children	Focusing on the children's grades, their sports or their material needs	Making time to play, talk to and interact directly with them (Psalm 127:3; Proverbs 29:15)
	Being obsessive about their performance, appearance or reflection on you	Focusing on loving, nurturing and speaking to them of their value apart from performance (Proverbs 14:1; 18:21; Colossians 3:21)
	Believing that children should function at adult levels and shaming them when they don't	Knowing that children develop at their own pace and giving them room to be imperfect (Matthew 18:5-6; Mark 10:13-16)
Extended family	Allowing guilt or obligation to be the "glue" that connects you with parents and relatives	Being honest enough to draw boundaries when family members manipulate you through guilt or shame (Matthew 12:46-50; 1 Timothy 4:12)

Table 10.2. Interacting with Others (continued)

	Nonrelational	Relational
Extended family	Reverting to subservient or childish roles when you spend time with family or relatives	Choosing to think and behave as an adult whether family agrees or not (Matthew 10:34-37; 1 Corinthians 13:11)
	Cutting off all ties with family because they've hurt you	Looking for opportunities to interact with family, unless doing so is unhealthy or dangerous for you (Romans 12:2, 18)
The Church	Investing in programs, committees and ministries	Investing in intimate relationships with members of Christ's body (Romans 12:9-16; Philippians 2:1-4; 1 Peter 4:8)
	Always telling other Christians what you think they want to hear	Being gracious to your brothers and sisters but never lying in order to keep the peace (Matthew 18:15; Luke 17:3; Galatians 6:1; Ephesians 4:15-16)
The Lost	Seeing them as a strange and alien race, completely different from you	Knowing that you are just as broken as they are (Ecclesiastes 7:20; Romans 2:1; James 3:2)
	Seeing them simply as an evangelistic demographic	Treating them as people deserving respect and consideration (Luke 6:32-36; 1 Timothy 3:7; 1 Peter 3:15)
	Leading someone in a prayer, taking him through a program, then moving on to the next person	Knowing that a person may require five or ten years of your life before she is effectively evangelized (Matthew 28:19-20; Romans 15:1-2; Galatians 6:2; Ephesians 4:2; 1 Thessalonians 5:14)

true whether those relationships are with spouses, family or friends.

When I was sixteen, I surrendered my life to the Lord. When I was seventeen, I led my best friend to the Lord as well. After that, Dan moved in with my family for a while, then he joined the Army. We wrote back and forth while he was stationed in Germany. Upon his release, he moved to another part of the state and got work.

His relationship with God was wobbly (though I did my best to help him over the years). I introduced him to his future wife and served as the best man at his wedding. They had a child and a lot of problems over the next ten years. In spite of my attempts to help, their marriage ended in divorce.

Why am I telling you this? Because this is how long it takes to be relational with someone. Dan and I have walked together over twenty-five years. We've seen each other go through victories and defeats. There were years when we weren't very close and then we would reconnect again. I got to walk through the two years that he and his wife were divorced. And I got to see Jesus put them back together through remarriage.

Their family and ours have shared in the joys and heartaches of marriage, career changes and teenagers. Dan is bald and I am fat, but we love each other. Practicing the relational principle with him has been difficult yet unbelievably rewarding. When Scripture tells us to love and serve one another, it isn't talking about starting church programs. Loving and serving require real relationships—complete with bumps and bruises—that develop over the years. This is how Jesus loves us, and this is how we are to love one another.

RESCUE THE PERISHING?

Next to sin and Satan, the number-one reason the world doesn't listen to us is that we are not relational with them. I'm not proposing that we jump in and have as many beers as they do ("all things to all people," right?). That approach violates the relational principle because it doesn't give the other person what he really needs.

We can certainly have healthy boundaries, but we *cannot* afford to do evangelism from a safe distance. If we are to be relational with the people at school or work we will have to take risks. Most of us would rather debate homosexuality or creationism. That way we can overwhelm them with our champion intellect without endangering our fragile core.

We act superior to those around us and then wonder why there is such a lackluster response to our "message." When our Lord reached out to people, he didn't hit them over the head. He interacted with them in a way that kept their dignity intact. Notice how he treats the woman at the well (John 4:1-26). He acknowledges that there are moral problems in her life, but he doesn't shame her or jump at the chance to prove her wrong. He demonstrates a genuine love for her and a concern for her situation.

People continually tried to pull Jesus into political or ideological battles, but he never took the bait. He always brought the conversation back to matters of the heart. If only we could be so smart! What would happen if we decided to love and respect others first regardless of how screwed up they were? Perhaps they would be more interested in what we have to say about God. This isn't "liberalism"; it's the way our Lord interacts with everyone (including you and me).

My mother has a live-in boyfriend who is an alcoholic. I see the two of them at their home from time to time, but one night I bumped into Fred at a convenience store. He reeked of alcohol and was in the store buying even more. Fred knows I'm a follower of Jesus and a Christian counselor. When I saw him, I knew I had a chance to love him on the spot. I walked up to him in front of God and the whole world and greeted him with a handshake.

I felt genuine delight to see him, and I communicated that. I can only assume that he felt embarrassed bumping into a "holy man" while he was buying more beer. Shame had already worn deep grooves into his face, and I had no desire to add to it. In the five seconds that we stood face to face, I was determined not to let his sin or disgrace stop Jesus and me from touching him with affection. It was more than he could bear, and he quickly walked out of the store.

Years ago I might have scoffed, "Had too much to drink, have we?" I've since learned that shame is not an effective tool for evangelism. If the subject of drinking or sexual immorality comes up, I'm happy to speak about it, but sending a message that I am disapproving does little eternal good.

Where did I learn this? From a Savior who is still kind to me after all these years (even when I am stupid and sinful). His gracious treatment of me doesn't make me want to sin more. In fact, it's just the opposite. The reason some of us proclaim our moral stance so loudly is that we are afraid. Afraid that people might think we are as bad as "the sinners." Well, guess what. We are.

During the quarter-century that I've walked with Jesus, I've been transformed. I live a clean life and am relatively free of embarrassing secrets, but I know that a big part of me is still idolatrous. The closer I get to God, the more I realize that some of my brokenness is permanent. So how can I look down my nose at the person next to me?

Does Jesus pour his love and blessing on me because I come from better stock? I don't think so. I realized years ago that I am still being evangelized. There are still parts of my heart that aren't convinced Jesus loves me. It's out of those places that my selfishness and idiocy spring.

Everyone is in the same place. The Spirit of God is evangelizing us all—some of us from the inside out and some of us from the outside in. Many on the outside will never admit their hardness and lower their guard long enough for Jesus to come in. They will perish. But those of us on the inside (within the body of Christ) have our walls too. Throughout this book I've called them relational masks.

May we continue to let Jesus radically invade the private places of our heart. And may we serve as conduits for him to do the same in others.

EPILOGUE

This I Know

Most Christian speakers and workers have one goal in mind: transformation. They hope that those they minister to will be forever changed. I am no exception. But I am also a realist. I know that some women and men will consider their core beliefs and relational masks but continue unchanged.

Some Avoiders will think they understand their avoidance, then go on skirting the major issues of life. There will be Saviors who add the information in this book to their base of knowledge but change little about their hearts. They will go on rescuing, fixing and "ministering" to others so they don't have to look at their own aching soul. Some Aggressors and Spiritualizers will use these ideas to whack others over the head more effectively and won't ever see the walls around their own hearts.

Another group of readers of this book will grasp the subtle yet devastating nature of their relational masks and attack them with a vengeance. They will allow the Holy Spirit to search every corner of their hearts to uncover each place devoid of love. They will flee to Jesus in prayer as never before, and their personalities will begin to change. Friends and family will be stunned by the reversal and welcome it with a sense of joy and amazement.

This group won't last long, however. The old relational mask will reassert itself, and they won't catch it. They will begin "doing their thing," and people who love them will be crushed as they see the old intimacy disorder creeping back in. These once brave souls will conclude that change at this level is just too hard or unrealistic. After all, other Christians aren't dealing with these issues, so why should they? This book and the biblical vision it proclaims will end up on a shelf of dusty devotional guides and self-help volumes.

I picture one more group, however. Their revolution will begin more quietly. God will open their eyes to the sin in their hearts that once passed for spirituality, compassion or patience. They will see how parts of their relational masks violate the very core of Christianity, even though most elements of their lives are externally clean. This will cause a grief and foster a determination that will be God-breathed. They will learn through trial and error that these parts of themselves that hide behind myriad disguises will require constant exposure.

They will discover that they need others to hold them accountable. They will regularly consult friends, leaders and counselors who can point out when the old relational mask is coming back. They will pray and read the Scriptures with an eye to the deceptiveness of their own hearts. They will drop the ball, of course—sometimes for months—but they will pick it up again and resume the journey. They will understand with ever-increasing clarity that honest relationships with God and others are all that matter.

These women and men will make it their life's goal to slowly and wisely love their spouses and children. They will slowly transform their church or parachurch into a group that takes the same kinds of relational risks they do. They will be quick to admit their blunders to people in the office, classroom or shop and will make amends. The people around them (Christian or pagan) will at first be skeptical, then respectful, then teachable.

A quiet conspiracy of honesty will grow in these families, busi-nesses and ministries. They will produce a type of Christian that is rare and beautiful. There won't be a lot of them; they certainly won't fill a stadium, but something eternal will be at work in them, and they will do their share of damage to the kingdom of darkness.

They won't be as polished as other Christians, but they will be go-ing forward when others have long defected. They won't usher in the kingdom of God or turn their culture on its ear. They probably won't make a big splash, like those who've crafted their relational masks into a marketable commodity. But they will touch people—both now and in eternity. This I know.

APPENDIX A
The Seven Core Beliefs at a Glance

#1: GOD CAN'T BE TRUSTED
How we demonstrate this:
- by using drugs or alcohol
- by being controlling and manipulative in our relationships (I have to act in this situation because God certainly isn't going to!)
- by spending money we don't have
- by relying too much on credit cards or loans (I have to do this because God will never give it to me, or he won't give it to me soon enough)
- by living in constant fear, anxiety or stress

#2: THE BIBLE DOESN'T APPLY TO ME
How we demonstrate this:
- by not reading God's Word regularly (the Bible is just not that important to me)
- by a tendency to apply it to everyone except ourselves
- by reading it but not being disturbed by its warnings or comforted by its promises
- by arguing with everyone about biblical doctrine but not focusing on obedience

by focusing on a theology that helps us feel comfortable and superior without dealing with the hard truths of Scripture

by seeing the Bible as outdated or unrealistic in view of the twenty-first century

by continuing a lifestyle or habit clearly forbidden in Scripture

#3: I Don't Need Other People
How we demonstrate this:

by being offended every time another person points out one of our faults

by insisting on having only superficial relationships

by refusing to reveal our true self to anyone

by saying, "All I need is my family"

by relating to other believers in a way that never disturbs our comfort zone

by being content with a surface knowledge of others and letting them have a surface knowledge of us

by refusing to ask others for help

#4: Intimate Relationships Bring Only Pain
How we demonstrate this:

by avoiding those who want more from us than mere small talk or pleasantries

by sharing our virtues with others but not our sins

by giving to others but refusing to let them give to us

by sharing our bodies with our spouse but not our heart

by telling people what they want to hear instead of what we really feel

by avoiding those who are in emotional pain

by refusing to embrace our own emotional pain

by working for God but not taking the time to know him

by reducing God to a theology, belief system or set of ethics, yet refusing to let him touch us in any way that makes us uncomfortable

by keeping all our relationships on a level that contains no risk

by focusing on job, ministry, hobbies or projects to the exclusion of relationships

#5: ROMANCE OR SEX WILL MEET MY DEEPEST NEEDS
How we demonstrate this:

by buying into society's views about love

if we are single, by believing that all our problems will go away if we can just be married

if we are married, by holding our mates responsible for our happiness

by using pornography, masturbation or affairs to feel better

by feeling constantly angry that our spouse hasn't met our needs

by fantasizing about the perfect relationship or wishing we could have someone other than our own spouse

by giving more of our energy or devotion to our spouse than we do to the Lord

by believing we would be happy if our spouse and children would just get their acts together

#6: I MUST DO EVERYTHING PERFECTLY OR I AM WORTHLESS
How we demonstrate this:

by refusing to admit when we are wrong, or admitting it only when we are forced to

by holding ourselves or others to impossible standards

by feeling contempt for the weaknesses of others

by hating our own weaknesses

by being obsessive, compulsive or perfectionistic about things in
our lives

by being self-righteous

by condemning those whose beliefs or lifestyles don't live up to
our perceived perfection

by forcing our children to do everything right and criticizing them
when they fail

by feeling as though we never quite measure up to what God
wants of us

by living in a state of constant condemnation and guilt

by fearing that God will reject us because we aren't good enough

by expecting that we should do everything well, even if it's the first
time we've tried it

by hating ourselves for being weak, tired, lonely, sinful or unlovable

by not giving ourselves or others the freedom to fail

#7: IF I AM HONEST I WILL BE ABANDONED
How we demonstrate this:

by always putting our best foot forward and never letting anyone
see our weaknesses

by representing ourselves as having it all together

by admitting our shortcomings or sins but being general about them

by confessing only those sins that are socially acceptable

by telling people we will do something even if we resent having to
do it

by being sweet and nice when we are actually feeling angry or violated

by serving others and doing nice things for them so they will like us

by being what others want us to be, even though we know it is dishonest

by doing everything we can to hold on to a relationship, even
though we know it is unhealthy or outside God's will

APPENDIX B
The Six Relational Masks at a Glance

	ASSETS	LIABILITIES
The Avoider	Easygoing	Passive
	Not easily drawn into conflict	Refuses to enter important conflicts
	Unhurried	Procrastinates
	Likeable	Spineless
	Peacemaker	Fears taking sides
	Steers clear of trouble	Steers clear of change
	Not easily excited	Doesn't act until it's too late
	Tolerant of others' weaknesses	Tolerant of others' sins
	Lets other people shine	Doesn't "step up" when he is supposed to
	Looks on the bright side	Sees through rose-colored glasses
	Doesn't bother other people	Doesn't engage other people
	Steady	Stuck
	Able to step away from volatile situations	Runs at the first sign of danger
	Rarely controversial	Doesn't take risks
	Doesn't have a sense of entitlement	Won't fight for what is rightfully hers
The Deflector	Funny and quick-witted	Refuses to be serious
	Makes other people feel good	Nervous around people in pain

ASSETS	LIABILITIES
Knows when to lighten the mood	Jokes at inappropriate times
Can help others laugh at their troubles	Has a hard time being empathetic
Industrious and hard working	Too busy to look at real issues
Affirms and encourages others	Bombards others with compliments so they never take an honest look at *her*
Knows how to laugh and rejoice	Doesn't know how to cry or mourn
Pleasant and cheerful	Fake and disingenuous
Not easily pulled into petty arguments	Rarely intimate with others
Focuses on helping others	Avoids issues in his own life that need attention
Great conversationalist	Talks a lot but says very little
Can minimize the shortcomings of others	Minimizes her own sin and selfishness
Eager to help other people	Has little idea what people really need
Good at overlooking personal attacks	Explodes when suppressed anger comes to the surface
Quick to help with projects or committees	"Drops the ball" when she doesn't get the affirmation she seeks

The Self-Blamer	Makes an effort to do the right thing	Declares an effort a failure at the first sign of trouble
	Has great compassion for hurting people	Has no compassion for himself
	Sees the value of others	Sees herself as worthless
	Quick to praise the qualities in others	Quick to condemn himself
	Quick to take responsibility for his sin	Hopelessly pessimistic and negative

	ASSETS	LIABILITIES
	Passionately angry about the sin in her life	Passionate in his self-hate
	Completely free of grandiosity	Sees almost no value in herself
	Able to love others with passion	Attachment to others is a desperate attempt to find self-worth
		Almost totally focused on himself
		Believes that God finds her repulsive
		Sabotages himself consistently
		Assumes that difficulty, challenge or inexperience is a sign of her stupidity
		Refuses to embrace God's grace
		Believes that others have a magical ability to succeed that he doesn't possess
		Believes that the affirmation she receives from others is flattery or naiveté
The Savior	Deeply compassionate	Deeply codependent
	Eager to help others	Does for others what she should do for herself
	Hard worker	Feels guilty about resting
	Will give "the shirt off his back"	Becomes resentful when others don't acknowledge his magnanimity
	Able to get the job done	Won't ask for the help she needs
	Doesn't waste time	Rarely has fun
	Has genuine love and concern for others	Expresses love and concern in ways that miss the mark
	Happy to do for others	Covers her sin and brokenness with busyness
	Doesn't impose on others	Feels superior because he isn't "needy"
	Isn't focused on her own needs	Doesn't nourish her spiritual and physical life

ASSETS	LIABILITIES
Quick to alleviate the suffering of others	Interferes with what God is teaching others through suffering
Very competent	Very controlling
Sees the importance of doing his part	Overextends himself
Giving	Grandiose
Quick to help others	Almost incapable of accepting others' help

The Aggressor

ASSETS	LIABILITIES
Very capable at starting, building or recruiting for a project	Largely incapable of nurturing, caring for or affirming people
Very practical; understands the bottom line	Nonrelational; sees people as tools for implementing his agenda
Sees the big picture (from a utilitarian point of view)	Is blind to the big picture (from a relational point of view)
Sees the importance of workable concepts and the "right way" of getting things done	Devalues those who don't have her perspective or insights
Able to remove people who are ineffective or at cross-purposes with goals	Sees the completion of a task as all-important; people are expendable
Pours herself into those who are moving in the same direction she is	Will "turn on a dime" and reject those whose direction changes from his
Has a clear perspective about right and wrong, good and bad	Demonizes those who are more balanced and equitable
Confident	Arrogant
Highly motivated	Compulsively driven
Outspoken	Insulting
Accomplished	Lonely
Effective and fruitful	Sick and tired (physically and emotionally)
A competent self-starter	Has contempt for those who are weak or inexperienced
	Unforgiving and full of grudges

	ASSETS	LIABILITIES
The Spiritualizer	Sees the kingdom of God as all-important	Isn't comprehensive in her understanding of that kingdom
	Isn't a "part-time" Christian	Has little patience for those who are broken or spiritually young
	Sees the importance of spiritual disciplines and practices them	Judges and shames those who don't
	Believes there should be visible evidence of a person's spirituality	Defines that evidence too narrowly
	Values the history, traditions and language of the church	Largely incapable of thinking outside his unique Christian subculture
	Is passionate about Jesus' lordship over his life	Excludes Jesus' lordship over her body, sexuality, attitudes or family dynamics
	Understands that Jesus is the answer to every question	Afraid of questions and answers that don't fit his conceptions of Christianity
	Stands her ground on important moral issues	Demonizes those who have a different perspective or haven't grown in that area yet
	Sees the crucial need for evangelism	Has a hard time relating to those who aren't open to her brand of evangelism
	Motivates and inspires others by his passion	Is threatened or suspicious of those who don't respond favorably to his passion
	Is ardent about holiness	Is unfairly black and white in her categories
	Takes the world of angels and demons seriously	Blames demons for things that actually originate in him
	Confronts sin in others	Blind to sin in herself

APPENDIX C

Discussion Questions

Individuals can use this discussion guide, but the author recommends that you use it in a group setting. Working through issues like this in a group is always more effective. If you'd like, you can set up a group that meets for ten consecutive weeks. You can tackle each question or just one or two. The format is up to you.

A FEW SUGGESTIONS

- Resist the urge to say, "Tommy, I think you are an Avoider." This could feel threatening to other group members. It could also be a way of avoiding *your* issues.

- Describe how you think the material applies to *you*. Be courageous and take risks. Ask the others if they see these traits in you and ask them to give examples. You may even ask the group if they think another relational mask fits you more accurately.

- Be kind in answering each other's questions. Don't attack or diagnose each other. If someone asks for feedback, answer his questions in a respectful way (remembering that it will be your turn next).

- If someone feels hurt or angry by something said in the group, back off. It isn't your job to convince her; the Holy Spirit has to do that.

- Ask group members how they would like to be prayed for as a result of the discussion. Each person can pray for someone else in the group. Be careful not to preach or counsel as you pray. Simply lift up the other person's stated request and pray blessing upon him.

I recommend that these guidelines be read to the group each week. Let them serve as the "rules of engagement" during your times together.

CHAPTER 1: THE STRONGHOLD OF RELATIONAL MASKS

1. At the beginning of the chapter, the author introduces the concept of relational masks. Which mask(s) did you identify with? How do you act this out in your relationships? Did any relational mask remind you of someone you know (take care not to use names or turn this into a gossip session)? Describe how the relational masks you identified may hinder your relationship with God and others.

2. The author says that 2 Corinthians 10:2-5 and Romans 12:2 are describing the same thing. Do you agree? Why or why not?

3. Some believe the Corinthians passage describes the demonic. If one person saw it this way and another person saw it as a description of the heart, how would their respective approaches to change and growth be different? Explain.

CHAPTER 2: THE FOUNDATION OF RELATIONAL MASKS: CORE BELIEFS

1. Which of the core beliefs best describe your way of thinking? How can a person determine what his or her core beliefs are?

2. On page 33 the author talks about "romantic orthodoxy." Do you agree with his conclusions? Explain your answer. How would two couples be different if one couple embraced romantic orthodoxy and the other couple didn't? Give examples.

3. Appendix A lists each core belief and how it is demonstrated. Identify which ones you struggle with (limit it to two or three). Determine to contradict these beliefs in the coming week and have the group ask you how it went. Note: For the purpose of accountability, someone may want to record each person's name

and the core belief(s) he will be addressing that week.

CHAPTER 3: THE AVOIDER: *SMOLDERING REBEL*

1. Take a look at the sidebars "You might be an Avoider if . . ." and "Things Avoiders say," and write your initials next to the lines that apply to you. If these describe someone you know, write her initials as well. Note: Include others for the purpose of clarification *not* for the purpose of changing the focus.

2. On pages 50-53 the author describes how Cynthia woke up to the changes she needed to make in her life. If you found out that you had only six months to live, what changes would *you* make in your relationships? Tell the group what that might look like. Suggestion: You don't have to wait until you get a terminal disease before you take action.

3. Look at the "Tips for Avoiders" on page 55. Mark the ones you feel the Holy Spirit is speaking to you about. Tell the group why you need to act on these.

4. Look at the list of assets and liabilities in Appendix B. What changes can you make to minimize your liabilities and maximize your assets? Write down what you will do differently in your family, job or ministry. Suggestion: This can be done on the back of a card that you keep in your pocket or purse.

CHAPTER 4: THE DEFLECTOR: *CARDIOPHOBIC*

1. Take a look at the sidebars and write your initials next to the lines that apply to you. If these describe someone you know, write his initials as well.

2. The author says that Deflectors either distract with humor or distract by focusing on someone else. Can you identify with either of these? Explain. Have group members look up the Scriptures listed

on page 61 after "The fact is, her sins are just as serious." How do these apply to you (Deflector or not)?

3. Look at the "Tips for Deflectors" on page 66. Mark the ones you feel the Holy Spirit is speaking to you about. Tell the group why you need to act on these.

4. Look at the list of assets and liabilities in Appendix B. What changes can you make to minimize your liabilities and maximize your assets? Write down what you will do differently in your family, job or ministry. Make it brief and to the point.

CHAPTER 5: THE SELF-BLAMER: WORSHIPER OF THE DARKNESS

1. Take a look at the sidebars and write your initials next to the lines that apply to you. If these describe someone you know, write her initials as well.

2. Do you see differences between conviction, condemnation and being a Self-Blamer? If so, what are they? Where does each one lead?

3. On page 68 the author says that the shame and inner pain of the Self-Blamer are real. But he also says there is a dark side to it. What does he mean by this? Explain.

4. On pages 77-81 the author says that hate is a Christian virtue. Does this sound right to you? How does the author suggest that hate be expressed constructively? Give examples of appropriate and inappropriate expressions of hate.

CHAPTER 6: THE SAVIOR: IDOLATRY OF SERVING

1. Saviors are often busy and helpful, but their effort inevitably leads to frustration. Why is this? Explain.

2. Saviors see *their* needs and the needs of *others* very differently. Why is this? What are the basic assumptions Saviors operate from?

3. If you have traits in common with the Savior, tell the group what that looks like for you. What would a healthier approach look like?

4. Look at "Tips for Saviors" on pages 96-97 and the liabilities listed in Appendix B. Mark the ones that are problem areas for you. Tell the group what specific actions you will take in the coming week to break these patterns. Ask the group for their input.

CHAPTER 7: THE AGGRESSOR: *HOSTILITY AS A SHIELD*

1. On pages 98-100 the author introduces us to William, a rather hostile Aggressor. What are some of the beliefs that fuel this type of hostility? Explain how this feels to the Aggressor. Also explain how it feels to the person on the receiving end. What do both of them need to understand?

2. On page 110 the author compares the Aggressor to an unbroken horse. What is a horse capable of in its wild state? What is it capable of when it is tamed? Apply this to the Aggressor and explain the differences and results.

3. Are you an Aggressor? If so, tell the group how this has played out in your life and what the consequences have been. If you aren't an Aggressor, describe to the group someone who is. What kind of fruit has her life produced? Note: If you describe someone else, remember to be kind in your description and keep his identity anonymous.

4. Look at "Tips for Aggressors" on pages 113-14 and the liabilities listed in Appendix B. Mark the ones that are problem areas for you. Tell the group what specific actions you will take in the coming week to break these patterns. Ask the group for their input.

CHAPTER 8: THE SPIRITUALIZER: *GOD AS A MASK*

1. To the naked eye, Spiritualizers may appear to be nothing more than hypocrites. Is this a fair appraisal? Look at Rhonda's story on pages 115-17. What insights does it give you about the inner world of the Spiritualizer?

2. On pages 119-25 the different types of Spiritualizers are described. Tell the group what these categories are and give examples. Note: Be charitable in your answers.

3. Have you been a Spiritualizer in the past? Tell the group what that looked like. Do you see traits of the Spiritualizer in your present? Dare to tell the group what that looks like now. Take a bigger risk and ask the group to share with you what they observe when you are functioning as a Spiritualizer. Be open to their feedback.

4. Look at the "Tips for Spiritualizers" on pages 131-32 and the liabilities listed in Appendix B. Mark the ones that are problem areas for you. Tell the group what specific actions you will take in the coming week to break these patterns. Let them hold you accountable.

CHAPTER 9: THE SECRET TO LIFE WITH GOD

1. The author says the relational principle is key to God's nature and everything he does (p. 136). Do you agree or disagree? Explain why. Have each member of the group name something God does (for example, causing the sun to rise, filling people with his Spirit) and let the group explain how the relational principle is at work in these events.

2. Those who struggle with a relational mask have unique things to overcome in order to be close to God. Give examples of what this would look like for the Avoider, Deflector and so on.

3. Table 9.1 gives examples of interacting with God in ways that are

relational and nonrelational. Review these as a group and read the corresponding Scriptures. If you agree or disagree, share your thoughts with the group. Note: Don't be afraid of lively debate; just be respectful in your tone.

4. Share with the group one or two changes that you intend to make in your interaction with God. Have them ask you how it went on the following week.

CHAPTER 10: THE SECRET TO LIFE WITH OTHERS

1. Table 10.1 shows how to interact with ourselves in ways that are relational or nonrelational. Review these as a group and read the corresponding Scriptures. If you agree or disagree, share your thoughts with the group.

2. Table 10.2 shows how we are relational or nonrelational with others, such as our spouse, children and friends. Review these as a group and read the corresponding Scriptures. Share with the group (from your own experience) how you are relational or nonrelational in your interactions with others.

3. Let each group member pick another person and share how she has seen that individual change during the course of this study. How have the other's core beliefs, relational masks or practice of the relational principle changed during this time?

4. Share with the group what you've learned about your own core beliefs, relational masks or application of the relational principle. Most important, tell the group what you've *done* as a result of this study.

5. Take time to pray for each group member, asking God to help her walk in the light that he is giving to her. Be open to holding one another accountable even after the study has been concluded.

NOTES

Chapter 2: The Foundation of Relational Masks: *Core Beliefs*
[1]Russell Willingham, *Breaking Free: Understanding Sexual Addiction and the Healing Power of Jesus* (Downers Grove, Ill.: InterVarsity Press, 1999).

Chapter 8: The Spiritualizer: *God as a Mask*
[1]If you have any doubt that doing good and being loving is the clear biblical emphasis, consider the following: Isaiah 58:6-7; Ezekiel 22:7; 34:1-4; Amos 2:6-7; Zechariah 7:9-10; Matthew 15:3-6; 22:35-40; 25:31-40; Luke 6:32-36; 10:25-37; 11:4; John 15:12; Romans 12:10; 13:8-10; 1 Corinthians 13; Ephesians 5:1-2; Colossians 3:12-14, 19; 1 Thessalonians 4:9; Hebrews 13:1-3; James 2:8-9; 1 Peter 1:22; 4:8-10; 1 John 3:16-18; 4:7-12.
[2]See Genesis 2:18; Exodus 17:11-12; 18:14-18; 2 Samuel 21:15-17; Nehemiah 8:8; Proverbs 12:15; 13:10; 15:12; 20:18; 24:6; 27:17; Ecclesiastes 4:9-12; Acts 2:44-46; 8:30-31; 10:33; 2 Timothy 4:9-13.

Chapter 9: The Secret to Life with God
[1]See Genesis 4:5-7, 13-15; Exodus 5:22-23; Joshua 7:7; Judges 6:12-13; Ruth 1:20-21; 2 Samuel 6:8; Job 7:19-20; 10:1-3; 13:20-28; 14:18-20; 27:2; 30:20-23; Psalms 13:1; 22:1-2; 44:23-24; 88:14-18; 89:38-47; Jeremiah 4:10; 20:7-8; Lamentations 3:1-18; Jonah 4:8-9.

ABOUT THE AUTHOR

Russell Willingham began his public ministry at the age of eighteen and has worked in evangelistic, pastoral and discipleship ministries ever since. In 1993 he joined the staff of New Creation Ministries (NCM) in Fresno, California. New Creation Ministries specializes in helping those who deal with relationally or sexually compulsive behaviors. As executive director of NCM, Russell does individual counseling, group counseling, teaching and media interviews. Russell is also the author of *Breaking Free: Understanding Sexual Addiction and the Healing Power of Jesus* (InterVarsity Press, 1999).

Russell is available to speak to your church or group. He does keynote addresses and talks, as well as seminars, workshops and retreats, speaking on issues surrounding spirituality, sexuality and growth. His heart's desire is to help believers experience authentic living and deeper intimacy with Jesus Christ.

Russell has presented workshops at the Campus Crusade for Christ Conference, the Annual Exodus International Conference, the American Association of Christian Counselors (AACC) World Conference and the AACC Super Conference on Sexuality. He is a presenter on the AACC video curriculum on healthy sexuality, currently in worldwide distribution.

If you would like to get in touch with Russell or his staff, you can contact them in several ways:

New Creation Ministries
P.O. Box 5451
Fresno, California 93755-5451
Phone: 1-559-227-1066
Fax: 1-559-227-4182
E-mail: russellncm@yahoo.com
New Creation Ministries e-mail: newcreationmins@aol.com
New Creation Ministries website:
http://www.new-creation-ministries.org